INNER HEARING

HOW TO HEAR, TRUST AND OBEY GOD'S VOICE

JOHN BATES

For information contact :
http://www.elanipublishing.com

Cover design by Nehemiah Bates
ISBN: 9780578517223

First Edition: June 2019

CONTENTS

INNER HEARING

DEDICATION

For my wife Shelli and children, Nehemiah and Eden; amor vincit omnia.

FOREWORD

John Bates is a "profitable prophet" to the Body of Christ. We meet people for reasons, seasons and occasionally life-time associations. This of course is God's choice in our lives. John is one of those "life-time" people in my life. Three years ago, I spoke in John's church and experienced his prophetic anointing. I was very touched when he shared with me his revelation on "How to Hear the Voice of God."

Who doesn't want this in their lives? I really encouraged, nagged and pushed him to get this wonderful revelation in book form because I knew it would bless everyone who reads it. We each need this revelation and the ministry of this "profitable prophet" in our lives. This book will be a great blessing to you as you learn more about hearing God's voice in your life.

MARILYN HICKEY

JOHN BATES

INTRODUCTION

In 1941, Walt Disney Productions released their fourth animated feature; Dumbo. The story, however; was changed from the original storyline written by Helen Aberson and Harold Pearl. In the movie version, he was named Jumbo, (later renamed Dumbo) a baby circus elephant born with disproportionately large ears. The other circus animals found him cute, voicing he would grow into his ears. Unfortunately, their predictions were unrealized. Although little Jumbo ate his bale of hay daily, the only thing that grew were his ears.

In a pivotal scene, Jumbo, tripping over his ears, wreaks havoc in an act involving other elephants. He is then relegated to serve at the mercy of the clown brigade. They paint his face with a silly grin and put a dunce hat on his little head and rechristen him Dumbo. This is where the movie diverges from the original manuscript.

In the original story, Dumbo runs away from the circus in tears, following an excruciatingly cruel performance heaped on him by the relentless clowns. He is befriended by a dapper robin in a red vest named Red. Red is an encourager, mentor, counselor and friend to Dumbo. During a visit to a doctor, facilitated by Red, a recommendation is given to Dumbo that he is to fly.

Red takes it upon himself to teach this former baby clown pachyderm to fly. An old Chinese proverb says, "When the student is ready, the teacher appears." Obviously, Dumbo is ready as he soon takes to flight with the help of his gigantic ears. Red is there to help him navigate and perform intricate maneuvers mid-flight. With repeated training, Dumbo is able to execute loop the loops and somersaults high above the ground.

After his private flight school experience, Dumbo returns to the circus with his new friend; Red, in tow. Red asks him to hold back with his newly discovered gifting until the proper time. Upon the circus arriving at Madison Square Garden, Red signals it is time to unveil the surprise. In the worn-out act of Dumbo ascending a high ladder and plummeting through a net into a mud pit--it happens. Dumbo spreads his ears and flies before he hits the easy laugh. People are astonished, amazed and even frightened. After the initial shock wears off, Dumbo is a hit! The book ends with Red flying with a paper with the word CONTRACT across the top. They are headed to Hollywood!

If you picked up this book or someone gave it to you to read, you most likely relate to this story in relation to the spirit realm. Have you ever felt like you "heard" things others did not? Have you "known" things without knowing? Have you ever puzzled at an uncanny ability to even process what is going on in the hearts and minds of others? I call this the "Dumbo Conundrum." Your ears are there. They are definitely there. Too much of a good thing you may have thought.

Where God has blessed you and calls you Jumbo, perhaps you have attempted to rename yourself or even had the unpleasant experience of being thought of more as a Dumbo. Your ears (hearing) are not your stumbling-block, your lack of understanding is and who Father God created you to be is what needs to arise.

Paralleling the Dumbo story, the good doctor, with a seemingly impossible prescription of flight is your loving Father. He has never doubted you can fly! In fact, he created you to fly! Red is representative of the Holy Spirit in our lives. A wonderful encourager, mentor, counselor and friend. He leads us into all truth hidden in God's Word. He knows all the tricks and is eager to teach us.

This book will assist you in navigating deep inner hearing (learning to fly with your ears). Three falsehoods regarding spiritual hearing will come to light leading you to an acceptance of your unusually large spiritual ears. Outer, middle and inner ear spiritual hearing will parallel to God's sweet instructions through the Word. Lastly, a permission to fly and navigate in the heavenlies will bring supernatural promotion into your life. Remember, Dumbo had to sequester himself from the doubters in his life before he mastered flight. Let this book and the gentle persuasion and sound guidance of the Holy Spirit take you there.

PART ONE

THE PROBLEMS WITH SEEING

"Seeing is not always believing."
Dr. Martin Luther King, Jr.

Chapter 1

Seeing is Believing – Fallacy One

I'LL BELIEVE IT WHEN I SEE IT. How many times have you heard that declaration? How many times have you said it? This statement is lodged as a testament of doubt and unbelief and often frustration.

A husband has returned home after his second affair on his wife while promising to never stray again. "I'll believe it when I see it!"

Your cousin just told you the $500 dollars he has promised to repay you, for the last six months, will be the first thing he addresses on payday. "I'll believe it when I see it!"

The shocks on your car are just about shot, as you have punished them navigating the decrepit thoroughfares of your city. The mayor announces a new initiative to repair all the potholes by this time next year. "I'll believe it when I see it!"

Do you get the gist? Through disappointments and let downs of the past, we can develop a tendency to look to the future through a lens of doubt. We forget human nature causes us all to exhibit fallible behavior at times.

Like the time you told your mom you would keep your room clean for a month if she (fill in the blank). Or the time your boss called you into his office and informed you that your lateness was compromising your effectiveness on the team and you vowed it would never happen again. And don't forget about when you promised your spouse you would stop all discretionary spending until there was a change in the financial situation of the household. The response, or at least thought, leveled at you in each of these scenarios could have easily been, "I'll believe it when I see it!"

Using the Bible as our reference, the furthest Jesus ever traveled during his lifetime was to Egypt when an angel of the Lord instructed Joseph to flee the persecution of Herod the Great, who was intent on finding and killing the Messiah. Upon the death of Herod, again, an angel instructed Joseph to move his young family, this time to Nazareth (Matthew 2:13-23). Jesus was most likely four or five years of age at this time and the sojourn from Egypt most likely carried the young family through the Gaza Desert and up the Mediterranean coast up through Joppa and then east to Nazareth. This is a trek of roughly 400 miles.

Several years ago, I had the opportunity to visit San Thome' Cathedral in Madras, (now Chennai) India. Tradition tells us the apostle Thomas was martyred in that city. His relics have long been moved to Ortona, Italy; nonetheless, it was an insightful visit. The distance from Jerusalem, the last biblically recorded location of Thomas, to Chennai, India is 3126 miles. That is a long way for a "doubter" to travel in regard to his largest doubt. That is approximately 2,726 miles further than Jesus ever traveled from his home. Why would Thomas do this, and does he truly deserve the title Doubting Thomas?

The Gospel of John gives us three glimpses of Thomas the apostle (called Didymus, meaning "the twin"). In John 11:16, the disciples show a lack of enthusiasm in regard to returning to Jerusalem with Jesus upon the death of Lazarus. Previously, the Jews had attempted to stone Jesus and the environment was turning more hostile to his ministry. Thomas was quoted as saying, "Let us also go, that we may die with him" (NIV).

In John 14:15, Thomas responds to Jesus' news of going to prepare a heavenly home. Jesus goes on to assert they would one day reunite with him there and that is when Thomas responds, "Lord, we don't know where you are going, so how can we know the way?" (NIV) Seems like a fair question to me. If that transpired today, he would have most likely asked for an address to insert into Google Maps.

Our last reference occurs when the other disciples tell of seeing Jesus when Thomas was not present. In John 20:25, Thomas declares, "Unless I see the nail marks in his hands and put my finger where the nails were, and put my hand into his side, I will not believe." This, too, seems like a fair exchange. The stakes were extremely high for the disciples. Seeing Jesus alive after his death would change everything for him. This verse could just have well read, "I'll believe it when I see it!"

John 20:26-29 (NIV) concludes this narrative by Jesus materializing in the room the disciples were meeting in, behind a locked door. Shouldn't Jesus pulling a Star Trek transportation act right in front of him be enough? It was obviously jarring enough for Jesus to utter the words, "Peace be with you!" After calming the room Jesus invited Thomas to, "Put your finger here; see my hands. Reach out your hand and put it into my side." After Thomas responds to Jesus' overture, he hears the Lord say, "Stop doubting and believe." Thomas is convinced. Next, Jesus offers this wise observation, "Because you have seen me, you have believed; blessed are those who have not seen and yet have believed."

I want to walk in blessing. Therefore; I am to believe even though I don't see. Of course, you know, this is much easier said than done.

A few months before I was born, Magdalene Crocker, a missionary to Burma, wrote a song entitled, "I Don't Need to Understand, I Just Need to Hold His Hand." I have memories of my parents singing this as a duet in the small church they pastored in their early days of ministry. This song has come back to me many times throughout my life as I felt the need to "know and see" what was going on at the time. In fact, there were days of me scoffing at the premise of this song.

The chorus:

I don't need to understand

I just need to hold his hand

I don't ever need to ask the reason, why

For I know He'll make a way

Through the night and through the day

I don't need to understand

I just need to hold his hand.

The one line inevitably getting stuck in my head would be, "I don't ever need to ask the reason why." I admit, at times I am just like Thomas. I need to see! I need to know! I need to ask the reason why! Or do I? There is a great difference between "needs" and "wants."

Jesus told Thomas to stop doubting and believe. He is telling us the same thing today. Seeing is not always believing. There have been times I have seen the blessings of God in my life in wonderful manifestation and form. Then a problem comes up I can't handle. I want to "see" the plan of God before I trust. Remember what Jesus said to Thomas after indulging his doubt? "Blessed are those who have not seen and yet believe."

If you have ever ridden a roller coaster, you will understand this way of thinking. One never gets a tour or even a tutorial while waiting to board. You do see many posted signs warning against riding. These protestations include: 1) if you have back problems, 2) are pregnant, or 3) possess common sense. There is also a sign with a measurement for height that sometimes includes a weight requirement. You wait in line as you hear terrifying screams coming from those riding. Still, you wait in line. You have even paid to get on the roller coaster! Are you crazy?

If we were told God constructed the roller coaster, we would most likely be filled with questions and expect full disclosure. Some of the questions might include:

Why did you build this?

Have you ever built one that has failed?

What if the bar and seat belt come loose during the process?

Why do I have to wait so long?

Where is the roller coaster class so I can know the "Top 10 Pitfalls of a Roller Coaster and How to Win in the Process"?

People seem to smile at the end after screaming during the process of riding. Can I just do the final, smiling part?

Will I get sick?

What is your (God's) liability if and when something goes horribly wrong?

How much insurance do you (God) carry?

Is there a "I Survived" t-shirt?

We ask none of these questions at an amusement park. We simply "don't need to understand."

My father often referred to roller coasters as death traps. So, it was with curious befuddlement that I found myself in line with him at Space Mountain at Disneyland in Anaheim, California, when I was an early teen. We were on our annual family summer vacation. Space Mountain is a large roller coaster in an enclosed "mountain." I asked him to ride it with me expecting an unequivocal "NO WAY!" Yet here we were in a long line.

The imposing warning signs were posted at every turn. The screams were echoing throughout the chambers of the building housing the death trap. We just could not see it. That may have been the thing causing my father to trudge through the line. Out of sight, out of mind.

When we got to the front of the line, my apprehension was somewhat high. I had ridden many roller coasters in my life, but I had always seen them before I boarded.

As we entered our car and the bar and seat belt were tightened, a sense of impending doom seemed to possess my normally confident father. We hurtled off into what was unbeknownst to both of us. Here was new news to both of us, you ride Space Mountain in the DARK! Except when a random light would flash just in time to cause you to think your head was about to smash into a low hanging beam. It was about ten seconds after we plummeted down the initial peak that my father's full-throated prayer language kicked in. I'll have to tell you, this was surreal, to say the least. He vacillated between glossolalia and English shouting things like, "God, if you get me off this thing, I promise you I will never do it again."

This is all occurring as we are hurtling through space at undisclosed speeds, never knowing what is coming next. As any teenager can tell you, this was a sobering moment. "What were the people in the corresponding cars thinking?" Dad was loud. He did not really need a microphone when he preached. He had a booming voice. Years of preaching Camp Meetings and brush arbors outdoors with no sound system had conditioned his voice for times like this. I will confess, it is hard to problem solve at warp speed. I did have a plan that showed up toward the end of this never-repeated scenario. I scooted down as far in my seat as I could and as soon as the bar released, I bolted for the exit and ran. I ran like my hair was on fire! And then the laughter began. A hysterical laughter...Wisely, my laughter abated before my father disembarked from "Deathtrap Mountain." We never spoke of the incident. We both know it happened!

I have seemingly re-lived this moment spiritually time and again. I find myself in line with God. I can't see where we are headed. There is an unsettled feeling. He seems fine. He's done this many times. He's not sweating. He's even smiling. God and I are buckled and barred into this next test. It usually takes me about ten seconds to lose it when I realize the brevity of what is actually going on. I can't see! Except for, thank you, the occasional flash of light alerting me to things I was not even considering. "God, get me off this ride! I'll do anything you ask. Make it stop!!" To no avail. Up and down, sideways, slow down, speed up, upside down, up and down, etc. You know, you've been on that ride, haven't you?

I refer to these moments as "God's Love Traps." He lovingly lures us into these seemingly wonderful experiences of faith. Had we any idea to the extent of emotional turmoil and duress it involves, we would politely decline – and never grow and learn to trust.

Why do people smile at the end of a roller coaster ride? Two reasons perhaps, 1) They are thankful they made it, or 2) It was exhilarating. No matter the reason, usually before you know it, you are riding a roller coaster again (unless you were my dad!).

Proverbs 1:8-9 (NIV) says, "Listen, my son, to your father's instruction and do not forsake your mother's teaching. They are a garland to grace your head and a chain to adorn your neck." These two verses were often recited by me to my son, Nehemiah, during his teen years. He committed large swaths of scripture to memory as a child, but these two verses repeatedly proved difficult to recall. So, I lovingly stepped in, whenever necessary, to jog his memory. And let me tell you, it worked!

The Book of Proverbs is chock full of wisdom and understanding. Proverbs 1: 20-21 (NIV) says, "Out in the open wisdom cries aloud, she raises her voice in the public square; on top of the wall she cries out, at the city gate she makes her speech;" This is followed by a rebuke from Wisdom due to ignoring her loving advice in verses 22-29. Wisdom is relentless, persistent and faithful. Until she is repeatedly ignored....

Proverbs chapter 1 is summed up in verses 30-33 (NIV), "Since they would not accept my advice and spurned my rebuke, they will eat the fruit of their ways and be filled with the fruit of their schemes. For the waywardness of the simple will kill them, and the complacency of fools will destroy them; but whoever listens to me will live in safety and be at ease, without fear of harm."

There is a popular song written by Phil Collins and Philip Bailey entitled "Easy Lover." The song could have been written directly from the following scripture.

Proverbs 2:16-19 (NLT) warns, "Wisdom will save you also from the immoral woman, from the seductive words of the promiscuous woman. She has abandoned her husband and ignores the covenant she made before God. Entering her house leads to death; it is the road to the grave. The man who visits her is doomed. He will never reach the paths of life."

"Easy Lover" was released in 1984 and quickly gained traction and accolades worldwide. Here are some excerpts from the song:

"She'll take your heart, but you won't feel it
She's like no other
And I'm just trying to make you see"

"She will play around and leave you
Leave you and deceive you
Better forget it
Oh, you'll regret it"

And the bridge:

"No, you'll never change her, so leave it, leave it
Get out quick 'cause seeing is believing
It's the only way
You'll ever know"

The bridge holds an interesting, yet faulty premise. It was as though Wisdom were warning of this trap of the immoral woman in the two verses. The bridge says "seeing is believing" so get out quick! Unfortunately, in the case of the immoral woman, it is often too late after one has entered the "seeing." The "believing" is followed by the whirlwind of reaping, forecast in Hosea 8:7. Here again, the words of Jesus ring true, "Blessed are those who have not seen and yet believed."

The problem with "seeing is believing" is that we are not always able to see. Sometimes we need to trust. Sometimes we simply need to "hear." We will get to hearing after we dispel a couple of other seeing fallacies.

Chapter 2

I Can See in the Dark – Fallacy Two

"Light thinks it travels faster than anything, but it is wrong.
No matter how fast light travels, it finds the darkness has
always got there first, and is waiting for it."
Terry Pratchett, Reaper Man
(Discworld, #11; Death, #2)

N ELEMENTARY SCHOOL, I often fantasized of possessing the

ability to see in the dark. My Saturday morning ritualistic

intake of cartoons fed this desire. If some superhero could fly

and another could jump higher than tall buildings and still another could stretch unimaginably long distances without snapping, then why couldn't I see in the dark?

I was not particularly easily frightened as a child. From ages three to six, I shared a bedroom with my little sister in the church's two-bedroom parsonage. I was her night guardian. When I was in the first grade, my parents accepted a new pastoral assignment, and we moved into a two story four-bedroom house. The house felt at least three times as big as the one we left behind. My sister and I now had our own bedrooms directly across the hall from my parents' room. This was a joy in the daylight hours, but something changed in me when it got dark outside.

For some reason, I developed the belief that a monster inhabited the space beneath my bed. This caused a great deal of anxiety in my life. I eventually confessed this deep fear to my mother, and she assured me nothing lived under my bed. She repeatedly showed me the clear space beneath my bed in the daytime, and then she would show me the same space at nighttime. She was quite convincing, and the lack of a materialized monster bolstered her case immensely.

My long-suffering mother repeatedly prayed with me, showing me the space and constantly reassuring me nothing dangerous was lurking in any part of my room. Eventually she came to the conclusion that I must confront my fear. She did this incrementally. First, she stood at the doorway, allowing me to walk to my bed and then turning off my light. The next step included her standing at the doorway but involved me turning out the light and walking to my bed by myself. The instructions she gave me for the final solution caused a quaking deep inside me. I was to turn off the light and get into bed by myself, without the oversight of my mother/protector.

I had a few days before this horrific incident was to unfold. This is where my track and field practice began. If this was going to happen, I was to be prepared. In the daylight hours, after school, I stood at my door and imagined walking to my bed in the dark, all alone. Then it hit me: I could jump to my bed if I got a running start. This also involved flipping off the light switch as I darted past it, mid-air. My feet would only touch the floor twice, away from the guessed wingspan of the offending creature playing scare-tactics under my place of intended rest.

My bedroom was over the kitchen and one day my mother came to inquire as to the scurrying and bounding noises she heard overhead. I explained my brilliant plan and she went back downstairs. (As a parent, I now understand that look of unbelievable resignation that came over her face as I gave her my foolproof solution to evading the obvious monster under my bed.)

The night finally came. My mother walked me to my door, prayed with me, told me goodnight, and walked away. This was it! Just me and the monster. I psyched myself up and took a few steps back from my door. My little legs began to move, and I leapt and hit the light switch. Something happened the moment I hit the switch. I had only practiced in the daylight hours with the light on and the sun streaming through my bedroom window. I'm not sure my feet even hit the floor twice. This was by far the fastest I had achieved my quest. I had never remembered my room quite that dark....

In the Apostle Paul's second letter to the Church at Corinth, he addresses the duality of flesh and spirit we must learn to live with as followers of Christ. He gave a wonderful entreaty in his letter which could find a sticking point in today's youth-obsessed culture. 2 Corinthians 4:16-18 (NIV) reads, "Therefore we do not lose heart. Though outwardly we are wasting away, yet inwardly we are being renewed day by day. For our light and momentary troubles are achieving for us an eternal glory that far outweighs them all. So, we fix our eyes not on what is seen, but on what is unseen, since what is seen is temporary, but what is unseen is eternal."

On our first trip to Europe, my wife and I were somewhere in the south of France and boarded an elevator with two octogenarian Italian couples. The men looked every bit their age. The Mediterranean sun had taken its toll. Deep fissures, cracks and crevices dotted the landscape of their faces. Keep in mind, Botox had not yet been approved in the U.S. at this time, so what we witnessed next was both startling and grotesquely entertaining.

The two couples were together and the animated Italian language, along with elaborate hand gestures, commenced. These people were enjoying life. They laughed unashamedly, and two of the four even had expressions on their faces while doing so. Something was not right. The ladies were laughing loudly, but nothing moved on their faces. NOTHING! Doctors have since learned to disperse Botox in such a way as to diminish the effects of the face looking "frozen." Their doctors had obviously not achieved this technique, and Shelli and I were spellbound.

I had to quickly look at their arms, hands and necks to regain my bearings. Yes, the bodies were aging, but the faces were not. This is what Paul was speaking of. There is a next for the child of God.

1 Corinthians chapter 13 is referred to universally as the "love chapter." Paul parks this powerful word between his description of the nine spiritual gifts given to the Body of Christ to bring about unity in a celebration of diversity (1 Cor. 12) and then the proper exercise of those gifts for the maintenance of order in worship settings (1 Cor. 14).

Verse 12 of the 13th chapter reads, "Now I see through a glass, darkly; but then face to face: now I know in part but then I shall know even as I am also known" (NIV). He was alluding to the imperfect mirrors of ancient times usually made of polished metal and sometimes horn. These mirrors gave a distorted view of a person's image as opposed to people seeing each other in heaven face-to-face and being known as spirit as God knows us.

In my teen years, my friends and I loved to go to haunted houses around Halloween. This is before the Church had a healthy understanding of this dark holiday. We literally paid money to receive ministry from the spirit of fear! One year I felt I had outgrown the fear sensation of the haunted houses. There is an old saying, "If you've been to one cave, you've been to them all." This was the jaded state of my late teen years regarding these bastions of mayhem.

My friends and I went to one of the haunted houses we had been to in previous years. "Familiarity breeds contempt" and my familiarity transfers to boredom quite quickly at times. I knew where we were going because I had been there before. What the haunted house had going for it was darkness. Had I night goggles or literal cat eyes, it would have proved no problem. In the dark, things feel different than in the light. A hand on your ankle when you can't see it is intimidating. We were toward the end of this particular attraction, and I knew we were headed for the "big scare" at the end. This is where everyone was herded into a room and left in the quiet darkness until strobe lights would begin to blink rapidly, and monsters in the corners of the room would lurch at you.

I remembered something from the year before. I had seen a light switch on the wall by the door. This year things would change. My memory was correct. We were escorted into a dark room by a menacing man with a chainsaw with an extraordinarily loud motor. He slammed the door and we were left in the dark silence to ponder our fate.

I found the light switch! I have never seen such disappointed ghosts, goblins and witches as when the light came on. Their sadness quickly morphed into aggravation and stress. It was too late! We were all laughing uncontrollably. When the strobe lights came on at their appointed time, I turned the light back off, and we danced wildly with the angry cast of fearmongers.

If life were but that easy. When things are dark and scary, we would simply reach over and flip the switch. We would laugh at the demons tormenting us and dance with abandon, free of fear. Life actually can resemble this when we realize how it all works. We need him to be our light. In fact, Psalm 119:105 (NIV) states, "Your word is a lamp for my feet, a light on my path." We can't actually see very well at night. Our natural eyes are not nocturnally proficient. Artificial means, whether it is a lantern, flashlight, light on our phone, or even a primitive torch are needed to compensate for our lack of depth and detail perception in the dark. Thankfully, God gave us the moon and the stars, but sometimes clouds cover them, or the moon is in its waning cycle. That is especially when we need added light.

In regard to walking down an unlit path at night, in the illustration the psalmist used in Psalm 119, only the path in front of us is illuminated. At best, we can only see the next few steps ahead. Have you ever considered how interesting things would progress if there were no night? What if we possessed hand-held tools bringing complete brightness at least 500 yards in all directions around us? Imagine the compromise it would heap upon our circadian systems. There is a reason for Genesis 1:3-5, where God created light, divided it from darkness and called the light Day and the darkness Night. He meant for us to have down time, to rest.

A few years ago, I visited one of the late-night prayer services at Yoido Full Gospel Church in Seoul, South Korea. This is the largest megachurch in the world and at the time close to one million members called it their home. I attended the 10pm to midnight slot with a missionary friend. Thousands of people filled the auditorium, and as we left, thousands were clamoring to get into the next service. We boarded a subway and headed to Dongdaemun Market. It was a Friday night and the later (or actually earlier in the morning) it got, the more vibrant things became. After midnight thousands of yellow tents opened up around the numerous shopping malls, all plying their endless rows of fashion goods. At 1am the Wholesale Clothing Town opened with hundreds of people streaming in as soon as the doors opened. After some serious shopping and sightseeing we were hungry. No problem, there was an unending sea of food stalls selling every Korean meal imaginable. We left around 3:30am and it was seemingly busier than when we arrived.

I felt it the next morning when we awoke to prepare for an early flight back to the States. Sleep is a good thing. Night is for sleep. God was definitely on to something when he divided light and darkness! When we artificially light the night and go against the rhythm God naturally built for us, we pay the price.

The point I am making is when we go through dark spiritual times and seasons of life where we cannot see how things will work out, we tend to ignore the fact that we cannot see nor discern the future very well while walking in darkness. We opt for artificial means of "seeing." Some resort to counseling from a secular mindset, others read leadership books to "lead" themselves out of the darkness. Others may solicit advice from as many people as will listen while another group of people opt for calming techniques. The more desperate we are to see in the dark, the more irrational our reactions. An unfortunate reaction for some is to seek advice from fortune-tellers and mediums. This was the desperate attempt of King Saul when he sought the help of the witch at Endor as he was trying to consult the Prophet Samuel through divination (1 Samuel 28:3-25).

Isaiah 50 is a prophecy regarding Israel's sin and her stubbornness concerning repentance. The prophet was called to prophesy over Israel, and obediently, he did. Verses 10 and 11 reads, "Who among you fears the Lord and obeys the word of his servant? Let the one who walks in the dark, who has no light, trust in the name of the Lord and rely on their God. But now, all who light fires and provide yourselves with flaming torches, go, walk in the light of your fires and of the torches you have set ablaze. This is what you shall receive from my hand: You will lie down in torment" (NIV).

If you are like me, there have been nights of aggravated sleep where you tossed and turned, wrestling with issues beyond your control. Awakening in the morning with a sense of dread, knowing the darkness of your problem was not eradicated by the rising of the sun.

The truth is, we need to hear from God when we cannot see clearly. There is a deep desire within us to connect with our Father. This goes all the way back to Creation. The whole reason man was created by God was for intimacy and relationship. He desires to speak to us; to allay our fears and gently guide us into peace with his voice of assurance.

One more allusion to "I can see in the dark" comes through an American horror-thriller film directed by Fede Alvarez in 2016. The film is produced by Ghost House Pictures and Good Universe. As I shared earlier, I choose not to pay good money to experience fear! I saw the preview to this movie, *Don't Breathe*, and subsequently read the plot.

The movie is set in Detroit, and three delinquent teens target a blind man who has received a large financial settlement after his daughter is killed in an automobile accident. The teens mistakenly assume the blind man to be an easy target. They even watch him outside his house as he feels his way through the streets with his walking stick. Upon breaking into the home, the teens find out the blind man has set booby traps within the house in case an intrusion ever happened. A chase throughout the house involving an angry dog and a pair of pruning shears becomes even more menacing when the owner cuts the lights off in the house. The advantage of sight is now removed from the teen invaders, and they realize the occupant's other senses are heightened due to his loss of sight. The title of the movie, *Don't Breathe,* becomes apparent once they realize the blind man can hear even the slightest breath. I am not sure of the plight of the wayward teens or the inconvenienced blind man, but the message hit me while watching the preview.

At times in our lives, it seems the lights are turned out. What we saw before is no longer relevant. We cannot see the future. We are seemingly at a disadvantage because we have lost our capacity to discern what is going on. We literally and spiritually are not equipped to see in the dark. As much as we may pride ourselves in knowing how to navigate through life, when it gets dark, we are at a disadvantage. This is where the importance of hearing becomes so apparent. When we can't see, we need to possess the ability to hear, and clearly at that.

One of the last services prolific songwriter Ira Stanphill conducted was at the first church I pastored, in 1993. While ministering to our congregation, there were two stories he wove into his singing/speaking. The first story he told was of how the song "Mansion Over the Hilltop" came to him. The second story was a bittersweet tale involving his troubled marriage and divorce from his first wife, Zelma Lawson. The couple co-wrote the hymn, "Room at the Cross for You" and sang it nationwide. The song would crescendo with their voices ringing out, "Tho' millions have come, there's still room for one. Yes, there's room at the cross for you."

After the birth of their son and subsequently experiencing disillusionment with the ministry, Zelma began to frequent nightclubs and see other men. Eventually she filed for divorce, remarried and took up performing in nightclubs. Ira did gain custody of his child and continued ministry throughout the 1940s.

I remember the weight of the story as he conveyed how many were critical of his staying in full-time ministry during this time up until her death in a car accident in 1951. One day as he was pouring his heart out to the Lord, while driving to the church he was serving, a song came to him. When he reached his destination, he penned the words to the song, "I Know Who Holds Tomorrow." The chorus is especially poignant with the words, "Many things about tomorrow, I don't seem to understand, But I know who holds tomorrow, And I know who holds my hand."

During his tumultuous first marriage and divorce, Ira could not see his way through the darkness. He had to trust God. He needed to hear his tender, sweet voice. He had no idea he would find a wonderful wife and helpmate in Gloria Holloway, producing a joyous marriage. Nor did he have any idea during this season that he would go on to write 100's of songs that are still being sung worldwide.

We must all come to the realization that mankind was not created to function as a nocturnal animal. We need the light of the sun to operate in our lives at full potential. Neither are we nocturnal animals spiritually. We need his light to flourish. When we go through dark times, we must lean on our hearing to pick up the directions and peace coming through his voice.

Chapter 3

My Eyes Never Play Tricks on Me - Fallacy Three

"We only see two things in people. What we want to see and what they want to show us." **Harry Morgan Dexter**

"To the short-sighted, through the fog, God must be a monster." **Cross Jami, Healology**

"You cannot trust what you see when your spirit is out of focus." **John Bates**

ENJOY WORKING IN THE YARD. There is a sense of accomplishment in "taking charge of the land." It is a joy doing my part to fulfill the command of Genesis 1:28, "fill the earth and subdue it..." So, it was of no small concern when I began to notice large circular patterns of yellow grass in my fertilized and well-watered lawn a couple summers ago. A lawn service fertilizes the yard three times a year. I quickly ascertained they had over fertilized.

Upon calling the lawn service and talking to the owner it seemed he was telling the truth as he assured me there was no way they were to blame. "We do not fertilize in a circular pattern," he said. I took a picture on my phone and sent it to him. He seemed as puzzled as I was. He actually came out to take a look at the yard and could not figure out the circular patterns of yellowed fescue grass in an otherwise green landscape. It was not a disease and he ruled out an insect borne problem. The surrounding grass was a lustrous green, suggesting an adequate job performed by the sprinkler system. What could it be?!

I honestly gravitated back to my original thought. The yard was fertilized when I was not at home. I had never witnessed them adding fertilizer to my yard. These patterns were precise. They had to have some type of fertilizing contraption spinning the fertilizer in a concentric pattern. An inept employee overdid it in areas of my front yard. Time to find a new yard service with an honest boss who would own up to mishaps.

How did I come to this conclusion? By deductive thinking. The obvious. Even my gut reaction. This conclusion was covered on all fronts--until the culprit was exposed. One hot August afternoon, I walked outside at the perfect time. It was around 1pm, when I would normally be at my office. It was my day off, and I decided to stay home. It appeared as if a magnifying glass was focusing a ring of light over a portion of the yard in a perfect circle. It was exactly highlighting one of the rings of yellowed grass. I was startled. Where was this light coming from? I walked out to the street in front of our house and looked back to get a different perspective. The ring of bright light was hovering over my yard with no apparent cause.

Life can mirror this scenario. Have you witnessed a problem in your life and tried to come up with the reason it was happening? You pondered it, asked questions, perhaps pointed a finger of blame at someone, trusted your gut, and then deduced the answer to the puzzle before you. It all made sense, until it didn't.

There is an interesting story in Mark 8. Jesus performed the miracle of feeding four thousand people who had listened to his teachings for three days. The crowd was fed with seven loaves of bread and a few fish. After the people had their fill of the miraculous meal, the disciples picked up seven basketfuls of broken bread. They got in a boat with Jesus and set out for the region of Dalmanutha. When they arrived, some Pharisees questioned Jesus and requested a miraculous sign. He refused to give them what they demanded, got back in the boat, and crossed to the other side of the lake.

With the abundance of food left over from the miraculous meal, it was unfortunate the disciples had forgotten to bring any with them except for one loaf of bread. One loaf of bread for thirteen grown men is not a hearty meal. As the boat was riding the waves, Jesus spoke some truth to them. "Be careful," he warned them. "Watch out for the yeast of the Pharisees and that of Herod."

Don't you just love Jesus? He would drop these truth bombs and disappear into the hull of the boat, leaving them to grapple with what he meant. After much speculation, soul searching, deducing and debating, they came up with this winning conclusion: "it is because we have no bread."

Mark 8:17-21 (NIV) is insightful. Aware of their discussion, Jesus asked them, "Why are you talking about having no bread? Do you still not see or understand? Are your hearts hardened? Do you have eyes but fail to see, and ears but fail to hear? And don't you remember? When I broke the five loaves for the five thousand, how many basketfuls of pieces did you pick up?" "Twelve," they replied. "And when I broke the seven loaves for the four thousand, how many basketfuls of pieces did you pick up?" They answered, "Seven." He said to them, "Do you still not understand?"

So I did a little math concerning these miracles. For the first feeding, each loaf fed approximately 1,000 people apiece plus twelve baskets left over. For the second miraculous work, each loaf provided food for precisely 571 people with seven basketfuls remaining. When you factor in the women and children in these crowds, you can easily quadruple the numbers.

They had just come from an incredible outpouring of food through miraculous multiplication. This was their second such experience.

Jesus' track record proved their one loaf of bread could feed up to 1,000 men and 3,000 women and children with approximately 2.4 baskets of bread left over. Again, this was per loaf!

The disciples totally missed Jesus' warning to avoid pride exhibited by the Pharisees and Herod. Jesus could deal with that. Of course, he was willing to spend time talking with them about the leaven (pride) issue. He enjoyed teaching them new truths. At this point though, the patience of Jesus was tested. They heard what he said about the leaven (yeast). Bread has leaven (yeast) in it. Jesus must be concerned that we don't have enough food since we only have one loaf of bread, they surmised. How insulting to Jesus. They decided he was worried there would not be enough food to eat that day. Can't you just hear Peter bellow, "Which of you dim-witted idiots was in charge of the food today? Jesus doesn't need this right now. He has to put up with those rude Pharisees and I guess he's ticked off at Herod now, too. Good grief, get it together, guys!"

Doesn't that concept sound familiar? We see something we don't quite understand and begin to try to make sense of it on our own. We trust what we see, often missing the obvious. That is why it is so important to cultivate our spiritual hearing. Things are not always as they appear. We need to be observant and use our finite understanding to illuminate what we see, but we must listen with our spiritual ears to gain supernatural perspective (that which is infinite and beyond, with Jesus.)

We experience this need to rely on something besides our sight as we watch a magician. Card tricks have always intrigued me. Those skilled at sleight of hand make it challenging to watch. There is nothing quite as bad as a card trick gone awry, but when they nail it, the results are astounding. The whole premise of the trick is "the hand is quicker than the eye." Many times, this includes a small distraction or repeated motion to draw your attention away.

Life often replicates the sleight of hand technique. We see something unfolding before us. It is clear cut and obvious. We make a choice and then things seem to go sideways. What we assumed would happen simply changes, reverses, or speeds up. Distractions come at us in the midst of change, and we are caught off guard by it all.

Years of practicing shuffling and rearranging the cards comes together to give a fast-paced seamless performance causing us to scratch our heads and wonder how that just happened. My personal shuffling of a deck of cards is laughable. Sometimes the cards seem to have a mind of their own, causing me to look mindless.

The enemy of our souls has been practicing deceitful tactics and sleight of hand tricks for years. He is quite good at deceiving the unprepared. When Jesus completed his forty day fast, in preparation for ministry, Satan was right there twisting and contorting the Word of God. He is a relentless foe and offered three temptations to Jesus, even using the Word as enticement. After Jesus' three rebuttals to the craftiness of his opponent Jesus said to him, "Away from me Satan! For it is written: 'Worship the Lord your God and serve him only.' " Then the devil left him, and angels came and attended him" Matthew 4:10,11 (NIV).

James offers an interesting take on how to treat the devil when he comes offering things to us that look seemingly harmless. James 4:7-10 (NIV) reads, "Submit yourselves, then, to God. Resist the devil, and he will flee from you. Come near to God and he will come near to you. Wash your hands, you sinners, and purify your hearts, you double-minded. Grieve, mourn and wail. Change your laughter to mourning and your joy to gloom. Humble yourselves before the Lord, and he will lift you up."

You see, trusting what you see without listening to the Lord can – and will – eventually prove disastrous for the child of God. We must come close to God after the facade of a temptation is presented to us. Never trust what the enemy offers. He desires to "steal, kill and destroy" you. It is not enough to simply walk away from the devil. You must come near to God. "Why" you may ask? To hear his voice. That is when the purifying kicks in.

So how do you know when your eyes are playing tricks on you? Experience is a wonderful teacher. If I went for a drive on a long, straight road through the desert on a scorching day, I would not be surprised if it appeared the road was leading me to a large lake. That is because I have seen mirages before. I even have come to expect them on hot days in arid places. I do not panic. I know my eyes are playing tricks on me. I have listened to teachings on mirages and have read up on them as well. Sound teaching of the Word and self-study of the same does wonders to dispel the lies of the enemy.

Since I understand mirages, I do not pull the vehicle I am driving to the side of the road and wait for the lake in the desert to disappear before moving on. I know the truth and must act upon it. When I hear God's voice, through his Word, I must trustingly respond.

James 1:22 (ESV) states, "But be doers of the word, and not hearers only, deceiving yourselves."

Have you ever felt you were on solid ground in your thinking only to find you were totally disillusioned in your decision?

A few years ago, my son Nehemiah and a staff pastor, Michael, accompanied me on a trip to train young church leaders in the Transylvania region of Romania. I found cheap flights through Iceland, requiring a two-night stay there. We packed some extra thick sweaters, thermal boots, thermal underwear, and hooded parkas. We would arrive in Reykjavik, the Icelandic capital, deep in their winter.

Iceland is an interesting place. The cold is not quite as harsh as imagined and the natural beauty is stunning. My personal highlight was a trip to Gulfoss ("Golden Falls"), a waterfall located in the canyon of the Hvita River in southwest Iceland. When the three of us arrived, there was several feet of snow on the ground. There is a ridge overlooking the waterfall, and you can hear the roar of the cascading waters from quite a distance. The tourist station was closed, and the sign on the gate of the long trail leading down the ridge explained its closure for the winter. This proved to be only a slight deterrent. The fence was easily traversed, and down the snowy trail the three of us went. What a waste to come all this way and not experience the thrill, we reasoned.

Gulfoss was everything it was cracked up to be. And it was amazing how the trail lead right to the swirling waters. Right to the brink before it plunged 105 feet into a deep crevice. It was otherworldly. Snow everywhere, a continuous roar and the thrill of standing on the brink of disaster. We took several pictures and selfies with our phones before we made the trek back up the ridge. What a sight! It was not until we returned from our trip that I decided to look up pictures of Gulfoss in the summer months. I was shocked at what I saw. The spot we stood and took pictures was extended far out into the river. We had been standing on ice covered with a blanket of snow. I think my heart skipped a beat when I saw the truth of what we had done. It had looked so solid and permanent. It made for great pictures as we were amazed at how close we were to the deep, rushing plunge. I marveled at my callous disregard of safety as I had led us over the fence....

How many times have you experienced pain in your life because your eyes played tricks on you? Perhaps you even had warning signs in the spirit, through God's word or the ministry of preaching and teaching. Perhaps the Lord even sent someone to you to issue a personal warning. Still you moved forward because it "looked right."

God is so faithful to speak to us, if we will but listen. Isn't that what you truly want? To hear his voice and know you are secure in your life because he will never fail you.

I graduated high school at the age of sixteen. Because of my youth, my parents thought it best to work a year and save money before I went away to college. I was able to find a job at the Criminal Courthouse in Houston, Texas. The job was in an unairconditioned warehouse which stored court files. This was before everything was put on computer. These were old cases, some of which had not seen the light of day in decades. If a case came up for appeal, the court requested the paperwork and deep into the bowels of this old building I would go to retrieve it. After a two-month tenure there, I was promoted to customer service in the main building and then quickly rose to clerk of the 228th Felony Court. No one had ever inquired about my age. I was a hard worker, yet unprepared for some of the emotional goings on of a felony court room.

The clerk's job was to keep the court's paperwork on the defendants up-to-date. It was also the clerk's responsibility to swear in those giving testimony. Sometimes I was required to go into the Harris County Jail and meet with the defendants to find out if they needed a court appointed attorney. At this point, I was considering pursuing a career in law. I remember the day that changed.

After a trial, the judge would dismiss the jury for deliberation. This was a great time to catch up on work. I just had to be near the courtroom for when the jury would reach a verdict. It was always somber as the bailiff would escort the jury back into their box after deciding the fate of the accused. This was sometimes a life and death matter. The judge would ask the chairperson of the jury if they had reached a verdict. If they responded yes, the bailiff would retrieve the verdict and bring it to the judge. After the judge looked over the decision, he would pass it to me. This part ALWAYS made me nervous. I would request for the defendant to rise with his counsel and begin to read the verdict.

There were so many trials and defendants that I did not pay much attention to their faces. I would ask questions while taking notes. During trial I was busy with paperwork. There was always the next defendant coming from the overwhelmed docket of the 228th Felony Court of Harris County.

On the particular day that held a career forecast change for me, everything had gone as planned. I arose from my seat as the judge handed me the verdict. I asked for the defendant to rise with his counsel, and I began to read it aloud. This was a murder case, and I knew there would be an emotional outburst from at least one side of this charged case. The family of the defendant and the family of the deceased were both in attendance. There was a large contingent of media present with their notepads and pens awaiting. I had scanned the verdict; life in prison without parole. I made it a point to never make eye contact during these readings. It was too much. As I read the final verdict, there were shrieks and screams from the defendant's family. The bailiff began to move in their direction as the judge began to pound his gavel.

This was Texas in the early 1980s. Handguns were prolific and there were no security stations or metal detectors to walk through at the courthouse. We were trained to look out for emotional shooters in moments like these. As I was scanning the courtroom and watching the bailiff move toward the hysterical family, it happened. The defendant thrust his hand in his pocket and jumped over the table in front of him. He pulled out a weapon, later determined to me a sharpened metal spoon, and came directly for me. I was between him and the judge. I fell backwards into my rolling chair and hit the wall with a crash. The perpetrator lunged across the wall of my box with his attorneys clambering after him. His makeshift knife plunged through his case paperwork and made contact with the desk just a few inches from my leg. It was mayhem. The judge bolted to the far side of his box and yelled for more security. The defendant's attorneys had tackled him from behind and the bailiff was rushing to us. I was frozen in place. It was all happening so fast. We made eye contact. I wish we had not. I can still remember his eyes, but nothing else. I cannot remember any defining characteristic about him. His hair, his skin and height and weight are all a blur. If I had to identify him in a lineup, I am sure I would be confused. This is how we see horrific stories on the news of someone released from serving years in prison for a crime they did not commit because they were falsely identified and accused. I cannot trust what I saw that day because of the trauma of the situation.

Life is often like this. Things begin to swirl out of control quickly. We think we know what is about to happen, and then, surprise! Something else happens. What we were watching for and trained for is no longer the problem. We cannot trust what we see. Our eyes play tricks on us. In those moments we must have fellowship with the Father and listen to his voice. He is there. He is always there: ready, willing and able to speak to us.

Are you interested in knowing what the light circles hovering over the grass in my front yard were? I walked into one of them and felt intense heat. The sun was magnified as I put my arm in the ring. Where was this coming from? I looked straight up. Nothing. I walked around the circle, and then it caught my eye. A high dormer window of our house was catching the sun and then reflecting it onto the yard in a circular pattern. As the sun moved through the sky, the reflective circle moved with it. Thus, the Olympic ring symbols in my yard. This only seemed to happen when the days peaked close to 105 F. My eyes had played tricks on me...

We are now moving closer to hearing his voice. We have explored the three fallacies of seeing: 1) Seeing is believing, 2) I can see in the dark, and 3) My eyes never play tricks on me. We know we must hear his voice if we are to navigate successfully through life. The next chapter deals with learning to actually listen to what you are hearing.

PART TWO

LISTEN TO WHAT YOU ARE HEARING

OUTER EAR HEARING

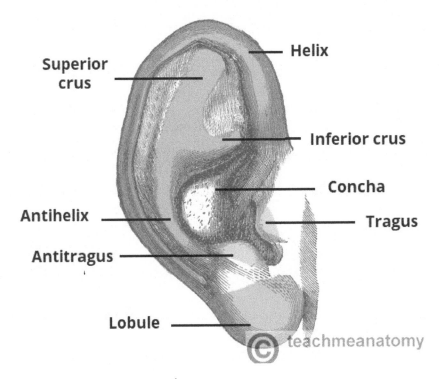

Figure 1[1]

Did you know that the shape of your outer-ear is unique to you? Much like your fingerprint, no one has an outer-ear shaped just like yours. This is important since we are making the connection between the way the natural ear processes hearing and your

---

[1] Oliver Jones, *The External Ear,* Teach Me Anatomy (2018)
https://www.teachmeanatomy.info/head/organs/ear/external-ear/ (Accessed October 7, 2018).

spiritual ears. Each member of the body of Christ comes into the Kingdom being uniquely shaped by their personality, gifts sets (spiritual and natural), and experiences. This means the way you hear is also unique.

Uniquely shaped ears run in my family. I remember looking at pictures of my father when he was in elementary school. He was a skinny kid with a toothy grin and large ears. He said the kids at school picked on him for them. Well, some things never changed. I caught a little flak also in elementary school over my ears. My ears have a little point on the tip, and I was called Dr. Spock quite often. I felt they were more elven in appearance but did not share this with my friends. They did not need any further ammunition.

The First Stage of Hearing

When we speak of someone's ears, we are generally referring to the outer-ear. This is actually the first of three parts of the ear: outer, middle and inner. Each portion of the ear serves a specific role and works in tandem with the others. The next three chapters will paint a picture comparing the outer, middle and inner ear to the three levels of spiritual hearing. To comprehend outer-ear hearing, an understanding of the physical outer-ear is necessary.

The medical terminology for the outer-ear is either referred to as the auricle or the pinna. The outer-ear is made up of both cartilage and skin. Three main sections can be identified within the outer-ear along with distinguishable features within the sections; the tragus, helix and the lobule. There is also a canal that connects the outer-ear to the middle ear at the ear drum.[2]

The auricle or pinnacle is the part of the ear that you see. Since cartilage and skin make up the physical composition, it moves easily. Go ahead, bend your ear, squeeze it and contort it. It goes right back into shape. The purpose of the outer-ear is to collect sound waves and direct them deeper into the ear. This is the first stage of hearing.

The question I am most asked by people in regard to prophetic ministry is, "How can I hear God's voice?" There is a strong desire to hear God's voice but usually the person asking does not understand there is a process and pattern to hearing God's voice and growing in prophetic ministry. Please do not misunderstand me and

---

[2] McGovern Medical School, *"Otorhinolaryngology – Head and Neck Surgery: Ear Anatomy – Outer Ear,"* The University of Texas Health Center at Houston (UTHealth): 2008-Present, https://med.uth.edu/orl/online-ear-disease-photo-book/chapter-3-ear-anatomy/ear-anatomy-outer-ear/ (Accessed November 20, 2018)

think that I assume there is an elitist pecking order in God's Kingdom where only his special few are allowed to hear him.

John 10:1-6 (NIV) gives some fantastic insight to hearing God's voice. "Very truly I tell you Pharisees, anyone who does not enter the sheep pen by the gate, but climbs in by some other way, is a thief and a robber. The one who enters by the gate is the shepherd of the sheep. The gatekeeper opens the gate for him, and the sheep listen to his voice. He calls his own sheep by name and leads them out. When he has brought out all his own, he goes on ahead of them, and his sheep follow him because they know his voice. But they will never follow a stranger; in fact, they will run away from him because they do not recognize a stranger's voice." Jesus used this figure of speech, but the Pharisees did not understand what he was telling them."

Isn't it interesting how the Lord compares us to sheep? Sheep need care, "The Lord is my Shepherd, I lack nothing," Psalm 23:1. They require leadership to find food, "He makes me lie down in green pastures," Psalm 23:2a. They are easily spooked by unfamiliar noise due to inferior eyesight, "He leads me beside quiet waters," Psalm 23:2b. They are easily confused, "He guides me along the RIGHT paths," Psalm 23:3b. Certainly, they need protection, "Even though I walk through the darkest valley, I will fear no evil, for you are with me," Psalm 23:4ab. Are in dire need of discipline, "Your rod and staff comfort me," Psalm 23:4c. Often at ease even though predators are nearby, "You prepare a table before me in the presence of my enemies," Psalm 23:5a. And, in need of an unctuous ointment applied to their heads to keep bugs, in our case; tormenting thoughts, away, "You anoint my head with oil." Psalm 23:5b.

What needy animals, sheep are! Jesus could have compared us to ferocious bears or tenacious raptors but instead chose the humble, defenseless sheep. We need him, and we must know his voice to follow him. We all start at this point in hearing God's voice. The only way to do this is to stay close to the voice we are to know.

In the days before cell phones, people had to make calls on land lines. Usually, you would identify yourself before launching into conversation. There was no screen to let you know who was calling. I remember a few awkward phone calls when someone would begin talking without identifying themselves. This meant they assumed I knew the sound of their voice. Sometimes I would have to ask, "Could you please tell me who I am talking to?" Their voice was not as familiar to me as the voices of my siblings, parents, or close friends. Those were the people who began talking without identification as soon as I answered the phone, and I readily recognized their voices.

Are you spending enough time with God to know his voice? In this age of mass media, we are inundated with multiple voices daily. Perhaps some of those voices are more familiar to you than the Good Shepherd's voice. The problem with the Pharisees is they were more familiar with the voices of religion and tradition than with Father God's voice. They rejected Jesus because he was simply saying what his Father told him to say and this was completely foreign to them. In John, Jesus goes a step further indicting the Pharisees by saying they were children of Satan because they listened to him and obeyed him. "Why is my language not clear to you? Because you are unable to hear what I say. You belong to your father, the devil, and you want to carry out your father's desires. He was a murderer from the beginning, not holding to the truth, for there is no truth in him. When he lies, he speaks his native language, for he is a liar and the father of lies. Yet because I tell the truth, you do not believe me!" John 8:43-45 (NIV).

It is interesting how we as believers seem to struggle to hear God's voice, but sinners readily hear and obey Satan's voice. This is the struggle of flesh and spirit. The Apostle Paul records this internal warfare in Galatians, "For the desires of the flesh are against the Spirit, and the desires of the Spirit are against the flesh, for these are opposed to each other, to keep you from doing the things you want to do." Galatians 5:17 (ESV).

.

The primary way to learn God's voice is to listen. God gave us two ears and one mouth. We should be listening twice as much as we are talking. If your prayer time is made up simply of you reciting things habitually and going over your latest wish list without listening for his voice, then you will never know it.

Another way to quickly acclimate to God's voice is to hang out with people who know his voice. Lambs are born to sheep which already know their shepherd's voice. Eventually they become familiar with the shepherd's voice as well.

There are two interesting stories about King Saul hearing God's voice and both had to do with his proximity to people who clearly knew what God's voice was like. In the first story, we find Saul has been assigned by his father to take a servant with him and go in search for some lost donkeys. As they approach the village where the prophet Samuel resides, God speaks to Samuel instructing him to anoint Saul as Israel's next king. Although Saul protests his new found attention by pointing out that he is from the smallest tribe of Israel and not worthy of Samuel's words, he is in fact anointed as king.

Samuel tells Saul that as he returns home, he will encounter a group of prophets. "After that you will go to Gibeah of God, where there is a Philistine outpost. As you approach the town, you will meet a procession of prophets coming down from the high place with lyres, timbrels, pipes and harps being played before them, and they will be prophesying. The Spirit of the Lord will come powerfully upon you, and you will prophesy with them; and you will be changed into a different person. Once these signs are fulfilled, do whatever your hand finds to do, for God is with you."1 Samuel 10:5-7 (NIV).

Saul did indeed encounter the procession of prophets just as he had been told. The Spirit of God came upon Saul and he found himself prophesying along with the others. Those that knew him marveled at the fact that Saul could prophesy. They wondered what had happened to the man they knew simply as the son of Kish. Was he now in the company of the prophets?

Our second story shows a very different King Saul than when we first met him. Although loyal to his king, David makes a name for himself in Israel by killing many a dreaded Philistine. He has won the heart of the people and Saul knows it. There must have been a deep understanding within Saul that God was rejecting him as king in favor of David. He had not obeyed when he should have. His demotion was his own doing, but instead of humbly accepting his fate, he sought to kill his rival.

King Saul sent several men to seize David and kill him, only to find that David had escaped. Saul learns that David has taken shelter in the company of the prophet Samuel. He sends men into Ramah to take him captive. But, upon nearing the house of Samuel, the men encounter the group of prophets and have much the same experience that Saul had initially. "Word came to Saul: "David is in Naioth at Ramah"; so he sent men to capture him. But when they saw a group of prophets prophesying, with Samuel standing there as their leader, the Spirit of God came on Saul's men, and they also prophesied. Saul was told about it, and he sent more men, and they prophesied too. Saul sent men a third time, and they also prophesied. Finally, he himself left for Ramah and went to the great cistern at Seku. And he asked, "Where are Samuel and David?" 1 Samuel 19:19-22 (NIV).

Saul takes matters into his own hands as he heads to Ramah in search for David. I find it interesting that he knew he would encounter this group of prophets. He had experience of that first encounter and what had previously happened to him. He heard the reports of what was taking place when his men encountered this group of prophets. Yet, he fully expected to be able to charge through them and get to David and Samuel. However, he was wrong. "So Saul went to Naioth at Ramah. But the Spirit of God came even on him, and he walked along prophesying until he came to Naioth. He stripped off his garments, and he too prophesied in Samuel's presence. He lay naked all that day and all that night. This is why people say, 'Is Saul also among the prophets?' 1 Samuel 19:23-24 (NIV).

We can safely say that Saul was prophesying through outer-ear hearing. He had real encounters with God. We learn that his heart was changed as he was anointed as King of Israel. He heard God's voice and responded by prophesying with the company of prophets. However, his hearing didn't change his fleshly issues of either inferiority or jealousy. Why? Because it was an external hearing that he never allowed to truly change his character.

It is not wrong to have outer-ear hearing. We all begin at this point when learning to hear the voice of God. Your physical outer-ear is contoured and multi-faceted with grooves, bends and folds as well as pliable and bendable. This is so the sound waves coming in different ways, from different frequencies, tones and directions can all channel into the ear canal and make their way to the eardrum. Similarly, there are different ways to hear God's voice through Outer Ear Hearing.

SOUND PREACHING AND TEACHING

Preaching is foolishness! At least that is what the Apostle Paul calls it. His preaching even killed a man. Acts 20 tells a story of Paul preaching so late into the night that a young man named Eutychus fell asleep and plummeted three stories from his windowsill seat. The preaching time quickly turned into the healing time!

Preaching is effective in getting our attention. However, if we only hear the words spoken and do not obey the words, they are ineffective to change us. The scriptures warn us several times concerning this shallow hearing. James 1:23-24 says, "Anyone who listens to the word but does not do what it says is like someone who looks at his face in a mirror and, after looking at himself, goes away and immediately forgets what he looks like."(NIV).

The first seed sown in the parable of the sower is built upon the same principle (Matthew 13). As the farmer begins to scatter the seed, the first batch falls onto the path in which he traveled. Birds quickly came to eat it up before it could take root. Jesus wanted to make sure his hearers understood this teaching. He didn't leave any room for ambiguity in its interpretation. He explained it. "1When anyone hears the message about the kingdom and does not understand it, the evil one comes and snatches away what was sown in their heart. This is the seed sown along the path." Matthew 13:19 (NIV). The way we protect the seed sown in our hearts as we listen to the word being preached is to obey what is being presented.

READING OF THE WORD

Deafness is not the only way to have a hearing impairment. Children who struggle to read often have perfect hearing but find it difficult to process noise correctly. This is called Auditory Processing Disorder. Although the issue truly lies within the brain's inability to process accurately (inner ear), APD is usually diagnosed at an early stage of reading development. The basic building blocks of phonetic sounds are never mastered, making reading a source of stress instead of a joyful experience.

We learn the basic building blocks of what it means to be a child of God by reading the Bible. I have heard it said that when you first start reading God's word for yourself, look at the Old Testament as the Duplo blocks that you buy for toddlers. They are big and chunky so that chubby toddler hands can pick them up and put them together. The New Testament is more like the huge, expensive set of Legos. It has all the little pieces that allow for intricate details and moving parts needed to create a more realistic structure. What was meant was that the Law of God is clear and easy to understand. The New Covenant, however, teaches us all the nuances of the Kingdom and requires a proper foundation to build upon. "All Scripture is God-breathed and is useful for teaching, rebuking, correcting and training in righteousness, so that the servant of God may be thoroughly equipped for every good work." 2 Timothy 3:16-17 (NIV).

If the phonetic building blocks of the Bible are never mastered, our understanding is under-developed. "So faith comes from hearing, and hearing through the word of Christ." Romans 10:17 (ESV). Our faith is strengthened as we build our lives upon the principles found in the scriptures, we consistently obey them, and we have testimony after testimony of God's faithfulness to his promises. We must learn the proper phonetic sounds of God's voice in his word in order to build the proper foundation that leads to mature faith.

EXHORTATION

A person who is just learning to hear the voice of God will highly benefit from someone around him with the gift of exhortation. This is a bit more than an encouraging word. A word of exhortation also carries within it a call to action. Paul exhorts those in the Philippian church with this, "Be imitators of me, brothers and sisters, and watch carefully those who are living this way, just as you have us as an example." Philippians 3:17 (NIV). There is weight to the exhorted word as it gives clear direction through gentle instruction.

Someone with outer-ear hearing may feel prompted to give a word of exhortation. When the Holy Spirit prompts us to speak to the corporate body, often that exhortation is not just for those around us, but for us as well. Father teaches us his ways as we share our revelation with other believers. When we enter into a relationship with Jesus, we become part of God's family. The body of Christ grows into maturity when we are able to entrust ourselves to one another and move in the gifts without fear of judgment.

TONGUES AND INTERPRETATION

The gift of tongues has certainly brought its fair share of controversy throughout the church age. But tongues and the interpretation of tongues do not have to be as mysterious as we like to make them. In Genesis 11, we read that "the whole world had one language and a common speech." Gen 11:1 (NIV).

Mankind aspired together to build a city and a tower that would reach heaven. In other words, they attempted to get to God through their own merit. God knew the capabilities of mankind as a united force, so he scattered the people across the earth and solidified the barriers by giving them new languages.

On the Day of Pentecost, that scattering was reversed. As the Holy Spirit fell upon those waiting in the upper room, flames of fire were literally seen upon their heads, and they spoke in unknown tongues. All of the nations represented within the crowd heard the gospel message in their native language. God was now revealing that Jesus was the doorway into true salvation and all men could be unified within the Kingdom of heaven.

Paul stated that he wanted everyone to speak in tongues. Now I want you all to speak in tongues, but even more to prophesy. The one who prophesies is greater than the one who speaks in tongues, unless someone interprets, so that the church may be built up." 1 Corinthians 14:5. Speaking in tongues can be categorized in two ways. One is a personal heavenly language given in order that the believer may build himself up in the Spirit. When we pray in our heavenly language, we give the Holy Spirit free rein to pray what he knows is needed. "In the same way the Spirit also helps our weakness; for we do not know how to pray as we should, but the Spirit Himself intercedes for us with groanings too deep for words; and He who searches the hearts knows what the mind of the Spirit is, because He intercedes for the saints according to the will of God."(NIV).

Where many get tripped up is that there is a corporate gift of tongues that ministers to the body that is different than our personal prayer language. This is what Paul is referring to when he says, "If anyone speaks in a tongue, two--or at the most three-- should speak, one at a time, and someone must interpret." 1 Corinthians 14:27 (NIV). The Corinthian church knew nothing about the orderly guidance of the Holy Spirit. They were all trying to outdo one another in the showiness of the gifts. Paul had to bring correction and explain that the gifts were given to build up the body, not show off the person. Where corporate tongues were present, someone was to interpret in order that the whole congregation might be strengthened.

One with outer-ear hearing can flow in tongues and interpretation. These gifts are sudden utterances from the Holy Spirit that are clear and concise for the people that are present. We mature in this gift as we understand that all things are to be done orderly – meaning being mindful of one another and allowing for the Lord to use all whom he desires in his timing.

Did you know that you can ask Father for the interpretation of your prayer language? I often have our congregation spend time praying in the Spirit. I then instruct them to be quiet before the Lord and ask him to tell each of us what we were praying. God loves to reveal his heart toward us. He is more than willing to let us know what the Spirit is praying on our behalf.

PROPHESYING

What an amazing thing it is to experience God's heart toward us through prophecy. He is not a God who is distant and uninvolved. And he truly desires that we would have an intimate relationship with him here and now. Father reveals his own character, his thoughts toward us, and what we need to know in order to maneuver the pitfalls of this life. He also reveals his eternal plan as he decrees from the throne what is done and what is coming to pass so that we might know that our hope is secure. All of this and more is experienced through prophecy – the inspired utterance of God that comes through the natural speech of man.

We have already seen that prophesying can begin on the outer-ear level. Our example was King Saul who found himself prophesying with the company of prophets, yet never allowed the activity of the Holy Spirit to change his character. During his second encounter with the company of prophets, the weight of Holy Spirit's presence was so heavy upon King Saul that the scripture says he stripped off all his clothes and "lay naked" in Samuel's presence. Now I don't know about you, but I think that is an extreme gesture.

The most likely scenario is that Saul took off his royal garments, keeping on a cotton shift. When Saul first joined the company of prophets, it signified being anointed as king. This time, even though he had fully expected to get his hands on David and kill him, he realized his kingly reign was over. Having come into contact with the divine utterance of prophecy, he could see his heart clearly.

Maybe in this moment, he knew that it was his own disobedience that had cost him – not David's charisma. Prophecy will do that. It will show you the true motivation of your heart.

Prophetic words need to be received in light of the truth of God's word. "Two or three prophets should speak, and the others should weigh carefully what is said. And if a revelation comes to someone who is sitting down, the first speaker should stop. For you can all prophesy in turn so that everyone may be instructed and encouraged." 1 Corinthians 14:29-31 (NIV). Again, when Paul addresses the Corinthian church concerning the edification of the body through spiritual gifts, he points out an interesting principle when it comes to prophecy. When a prophetic word is spoken, the others should weigh it. That is important. Someone with outer-ear hearing may certainly prophesy, but they may also lack the years of discipleship that it takes to walk in maturity. Therefore, they may hear correctly, but not know how to deliver the word in gentleness and love. Or, they may believe they hear correctly, but do not have the understanding to process the word through compassion. Jealousy, unforgiveness, bitterness, and other emotions that cloud our soul also skew our understanding of prophetic purpose. New Testament prophecy is to build-up, edify, and encourage. "If I have the gift of prophecy and can fathom all mysteries and all knowledge, and if I have a faith that can move mountains, but do not have love, I am nothing," 1 Corinthians 13:2 (NIV).

In the Old Testament, we often see God calling a single man to a prophetic office. In the New Testament, prophecy is given to the body. In other words, it is used to build up believers in the corporate setting. We see prophetic teams as we read the accounts of the early church's activities. In Acts 13:1, we see prophets and teachers working together to strengthen new converts. In Acts 11:27, we learn of a team of prophets from Antioch.

Interestingly enough, Moses saw the value of prophetic teams as he led the people out of Egypt. The burden was too heavy to bear alone. The Lord instructed Moses to bring seventy leaders in Israel together. This was so God could give them a measure of the Spirit that was on Moses in order to help him lead. The Bible tells us that these men prophesied as this took place. Two men who were elders did not attend this meeting between the Lord, Moses, and the other elders. However, they began to prophesy as well. Moses' loyal assistant Joshua was indignant at this, but Moses wasn't jealous. He knew that he needed others. "Joshua son of Nun, who had been Moses' aide since youth, spoke up and said, "Moses, my lord, stop them!" But Moses replied, 'Are you jealous for my sake? I wish that all the Lord's people were prophets and that the Lord would put his Spirit on them!' Then Moses and the elders of Israel returned to the camp." Numbers 11:28-30 (NIV).

It is good for us to remember that we should always prophesy with compassion. "Love never fails. But where there are prophecies, they will cease; where there are tongues, they will be restrained; where there is knowledge, it will be dismissed. For we know in part and we prophesy in part, but when the perfect comes, the partial passes away...." 1 Corinthians 13:8-10. Jesus is the perfect standard coming back for his bride. We won't need the spiritual gifts when we are in the presence of Jesus. But, until then, we prophesy in part. This means we have to be subject to others so that we prophesy in love. For those with outer-ear hearing, this is a giant step in growing toward middle ear hearing.

DREAMS AND VISIONS

A lady who had been around the prophetic a little bit approached her pastor. She wanted to appear educated in her gifting, so she said, "Pastor, I just want you to know, this weekend, the Lord spoke to me in a dream. I saw a heifer high and lifted up. What does this mean?" The pastor's response to the dear lady was, "Sister, the cost of meat is going sky high."

People with outer-ear hearing may certainly have visions and dreams. However, they typically need a more seasoned prophetic person to interpret what they see. This was certainly the case with Pharaoh's cupbearer and his baker who had been thrown into prison alongside Joseph. In Genesis, we read that both men had significant dreams the same evening but were depressed that they did not know what their dreams meant. "Then Joseph said to them, "Do not interpretations belong to God? Tell me your dreams," Genesis 40:8 (NIV).

Joseph was accurate in his interpretation of both dreams. Because of that, when Pharaoh was given a troubling dream he didn't understand, Joseph was brought before him to give the interpretation. Pharaoh, along with his cupbearer and his baker, were aware these dreams had significant meaning. However, they needed someone with middle or inner ear hearing in order to understand the message.

I often have people tell me about their visions or dreams. They are certain that they are from God, but the meaning of the encounters is not clear. Why would God show a person a vision and not make plain the interpretation? In Joseph's case, God was setting him up to gain favor with Pharaoh in order that Joseph might save his family from the coming famine. For us, maybe the answer is again found in the ministry of the body. Those with outer-ear hearing need to learn from others who have deeper perception. In turn, those regularly hearing from God need to be reminded of the wonderment of what it was like when they first realized God speaks in tangible ways.

AUDIBLE VOICES AND ANGELS

We tend to think those who hear audible voices or angels speak to them are listening with inner ear hearing. But there are many instances in the Bible where this was not the case. Jesus spoke to the murderous Saul as he was in pursuit of Christians to arrest them. Saul experienced both a vision in the blinding light and heard the audible voice of the Lord. This was pre-salvation for the soon to be apostle. He was not predisposed to believe that Jesus was the Messiah – on the contrary. Yet, when Jesus identified himself, Saul obeyed the Lord's directives. We can argue that Saul's conversion needed to be dramatic in order for him to fulfill his calling, but there are other instances as well.

We are fond of shepherds due to our familiarity of the nativity scene. Toddlers everywhere are the pride of their parents as they stand on the Christmas stage in their cute shepherd costumes. However, shepherds were considered men of lowly estate in the ancient world. By the time Jesus made his earthly entrance, shepherds could be found on the bottom tier of society. Early in biblical history, we see that shepherding was valued and respected. But 400 years as Egyptian slaves had brought with it a prejudiced mindset toward the shepherds of Israel. It was a difficult, lonely life, and yet, this is to whom the angels appeared.

Maybe one of the most colorful moments that God spoke audibly is the story of Balaam and his donkey. Balaam is an interesting character in himself. He is being paid a diviner's price by the King of Moab to curse Israel as they camp along the Jordan across from Jericho. Balaam actually inquires of the Lord as to how to handle the King's request. God's response is to let him know that these were blessed people, and that under no circumstance was Balaam allowed to curse them. Balaam's heart seems more concerned for the reward from the King of Moab than obedience to God's voice. Seeing that, God tells Balaam to go with the Moabites, but then gets angry as he goes. The angel of the Lord actually stands in the road with drawn sword in opposition to Balaam, but the befuddled seer doesn't see him. There is something which sees clearly, though– Balaam's donkey.

Three times the donkey detours off the road in dramatic fashion. Each time, he is beaten and chastised so that he might continue down the road. I wonder sometimes, if this was an unusual encounter or if animals can simply see better into spiritual things. What takes place next certainly is not normal. Balaam begins to fuss at his donkey, like we might expect him to do. But, to his surprise, his donkey talks back: Then the Lord opened the donkey's mouth, and it said to Balaam, 'What have I done to you to make you beat me these three times?' Balaam answered the donkey, 'You have made a fool of me! If only I had a sword in my hand, I would kill you right now.' The donkey said to Balaam, 'Am I not your own donkey, which you have always ridden, to this day? Have I been in the habit of doing this to you?' 'No,' he said. Then the Lord opened Balaam's eyes, and he saw the angel of the Lord standing in the road with his sword drawn. So, he bowed low and fell facedown." Numbers 22:28-31(NIV).

Does anyone else find it funny that Balaam simply answers his donkey when he begins to speak, or is that just me?

OUTER EAR HEARING AILMENTS

When we experience physical outer-ear pain, it is usually more of a mild discomfort. The appearance of the ear may not look swollen or red. We may not experience any visible symptoms other than a brief annoying irritation we try to ignore until it goes away. Sometimes the soreness corrects itself, and sometimes, it is the onset of something much more serious that needs medical attention. Either way, at the outer-ear level, we tend to barrel through the symptoms continuing on with our daily routines simply hoping the pain will just stop.

We do the same thing on a spiritual level. Our outer-ear hearing loss is caused by a lack of maturity. We do not know how to distinguish between truth and earthly wisdom. We allow ourselves to hear and take in everything that may sound good or make us feel good because we have not set the filter of the Bible in place. Do you remember Jesus' words in Matthew 13? The seed that was sown along the path is the word of God. Before that seed could implant deeply into the hearer's heart, the birds came and ate it so that it never took root. A person who is not grounded in scripture can be easily swayed by smooth deceptive words.

The remedy for outer-ear hearing ailments is found in learning how to listen with our spiritual ears instead of determining truth for ourselves. We do this by asking God to teach us wisdom through prayer; by studying His word and applying it; and through obedience. The apostle Paul was always concerned for his newly planted churches. He prayed that each member would grow into a mature believer: "For this reason, since the day we heard about you, we have not stopped praying for you. We continually ask God to fill you with the knowledge of his will through all the wisdom and understanding that the Spirit gives, so that you may live a life worthy of the Lord and please him in every way: bearing fruit in every good work, growing in the knowledge of God." Colossians 1:9-10 (NIV).

THE OBEDIENCE FACTOR

It doesn't take a lot of obedience to have outer-ear hearing. The goal is not to simply begin to hear, but to grow in the way we hear the Lord's voice.

It was thought that my great-grandfather, over the course of several years, went deaf. Those around him screamed at him to get a hearing aid. He went to the ear doctor, only to find he wasn't deaf at all. Heavy ear wax had built up, plugging his ears. Once the wax was removed, he heard fine. His only problem then was being upset when people still screamed at him.

Partial obedience is like that ear wax that won't allow the sound to reach the middle ear. If not remedied, a sense of deafness may occur. One of the first lessons new believers should learn is that obedience equals love in God's economy: "When we obey God, we are sure that we know him. We truly love God only when we obey him as we should, and then we know that we belong to him. If we say we are his, we must follow the example of Christ." 1 John 2:3-6 (NIV).

MIDDLE EAR HEARING

The Middle Ear

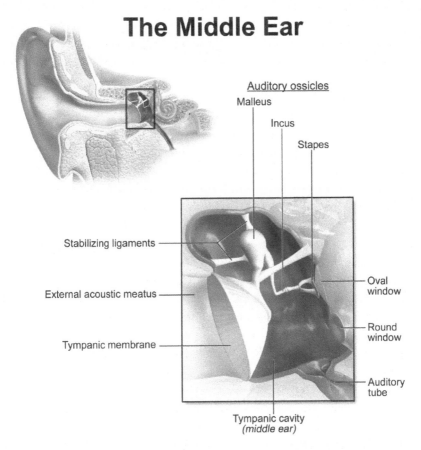

Figure 2[3]

The middle ear is classified as everything between the tympanic membrane (the ear drum) and the oval window which leads into the inner ear. In essence, it's a cavity that contains the pharynx, which is attached to the Eustachian tube and the auditory ossicles. The

---

[3] Blausen.com staff (2014). "Medical gallery of Blausen Medical 2014". WikiJournal of Medicine 1 (2). DOI:10.15347/wjm/2014.010. ISSN 2002-4436

ossicles are three small bones called the malleus, incus, and stapes. These bones act as the bridge between the ear drum and the inner ear. Your body's ability to adjust to motion (equilibrium) is also regulated here. However, the main function of the middle ear is to move sound vibrations from the ear drum into the inner ear.[4]

A competent electric guitarist will tell you an amp with a good acoustic transformer is needed to produce the right sound with clarity. The transformer is what changes the voltage in between the wires and the speakers. But there is also a process called preamplification that reduces the noise and distortion of the sound. If the amp is faulty, the sound is distorted. The transformer is essentially the middle ear of the amp.

In the ear, the tympanic membrane acts as a drum that vibrates when it interacts with sound waves. This motion amplifies the sound that might otherwise be muffled. Those amplified sound waves then travel through the ossicles, which help to bring clarity. From the ossicles, the sound waves travel to the oval window. The transformed sound is now ready to enter the inner ear.

---

[4] Hear It, *"The Middle Ear,"* Hearing Loss, https://www.hear-it.org/The-middle-ear-1 (Accessed May 10, 2019).

Like sound traveling through the amplifier, the person with middle ear hearing is experiencing the same process in the Spirit. The output is getting stronger, louder and clearer. The technical term for this transformation process is called gain. Middle ear hearing allows one to experience a like measure of gain in their understanding. This increased understanding happens both in what they hear the Spirit say and how they use it to benefit others.

HEARING GOD'S VOICE IN PERSONAL STUDY

The first time most of us experience spiritual gain is as we are studying the word of God in our quiet time. All of the sudden, we become acutely aware of God's voice as he opens up his Word to us. He amplifies the meaning of what we are reading and causes us to hear with clarity the rich truths laid out before us. Jesus alludes to the joy of this process in the parable of the sower: "The seed falling on rocky ground refers to someone who hears the word and at once receives it with joy." Matthew 13:20 (NIV).

Our hearts may still be rocky ground in the sense that the work of sanctification has just begun, but as we hear the Lord's voice amplify the truth, we receive it. In order to receive something, we must grasp it. We then take possession of it, making it our own. Middle ear hearing allows understanding to be worked into us as we learn what it means to be a true disciple of Jesus. We see Paul encouraging the church in Thessalonica to do just that: "For this reason, we also constantly thank God that when you received the word of God which you heard from us, you accepted it not as the word of men, but for what it really is, the word of God, which also performs its work in you who believe." 1 Thessalonians 2:13 (NIV).

PREACHING WITH SUCCESS

Preaching and teaching are distinctly different, and yet, not easy to separate. It could be said that teaching is establishing what is true, and preaching is encouraging others to respond to that truth. It is difficult to have one without the other. You can't preach effectively without teaching the underlying truths that must be built upon. And if your teaching is void of passion and the need to obey the truth being presented, what is the benefit to your listeners?

When I was nineteen years of age, I preached my first sermon. I do not remember the text nor the outline. I do remember many other things about that night...

It was a small church in Athens, Texas on a Sunday night. I had prepared extensively and imagined the content would last twenty-five to thirty minutes. I wrote every word out in large font on several papers. This is how my dad did it, so I followed suit.

I was more excited than nervous, although nerves were in play. That is not all in play that night. It seems a virus was also at work.

About halfway through my sermon, which I was delivering at lightning speed, one of the cute schoolchildren on the front row turned and vomited on her friend. I froze, but her friend did not. Her friend returned a volley of vomit in the original offender's direction. There are many things I can now think to do. Unfortunately, all that came to me at the time was to laugh. Inappropriate? Yes!! Everything stopped as mothers scrambled to clean up the crying girls on the front row. The other parents were hastily leaving with their own children. The crowd was not large to start with, and the vomiting debacle cleared at least a third of the crowd in less than a minute.

The sermon ended up lasting twelve minutes, including the unplanned intermission. Since then I have learned a few things about preaching the Word.

Maturing in the ability to preach effectively requires a knowledge of how to unite what we hear the Spirit say and what we study in the scriptures. Paul gives us a great example of this middle ear hearing in his first letter to the Corinthians: "Jews demand signs and Greeks look for wisdom, but we preach Christ crucified: a stumbling block to Jews and foolishness to Gentiles, but to those whom God has called, both Jews and Greeks, Christ the power of God and the wisdom of God." 1 Corinthians 1:22-24 (NIV).

Staying true to the gospel message is vital. However, the understanding that people come from different backgrounds and have varying needs requires that we rely upon the guidance of the Holy Spirit when preparing to preach. Like me, Paul preached in Athens, too. Only he wasn't in Texas. He was in ancient Athens which is now modern-day Greece at a place known as the Areopagus, or more commonly called, Mars Hill.

Several years ago, I sat on Mars Hill at twilight looking out over the city. Hundreds of tourists, along with many locals, joined me at this site to ponder the peaceful solemnity the place exudes. People were speaking in hushed tones, maybe in humble reverence to what the place represents – wisdom. As the locals sat there and whispered to one another, they shared loaves of bread, fruit, wine, and cheese.

Mars Hill was a heightened rocky plateau that served as a stage overlooking the market area. Acts 17:17 tells us that not only did Paul teach in the synagogues, he also "disputed daily in the marketplace." Greeks loved philosophy and debate. They would frequently gather in order to hear the latest wisdom being espoused by the philosophers. Paul seized the moment to preach the gospel by making it relevant to their Greek culture. Two differing groups of philosophers were present, the Stoics and the Epicureans. They were so enthralled by what Paul was saying, they took him up to Mars Hill so that he would have a platform in which to speak.

However, when Paul taught in the synagogues, we read he "reasoned in the synagogues with the Jews and the God-fearing people." Acts 17:17 (NIV). These were not people interested in Greek philosophy. These were people steeped in the traditions of the Torah, along with their proselytes. He still preached the gospel, but he pointed to the ancient scriptures in order to prove that Jesus was their long-awaited Messiah. There was an understanding in Paul that he needed to both follow the Spirit's lead in ministering to different people and explain what he knew to be true about the scriptures.

TEACHING WITH SUCCESS

I continued to preach on weekends throughout my years in Bible School. One weekend I was back in East Texas at another small church. There were probably forty people in attendance that day. There was an adult Sunday School class and a children's Sunday School class. I unwittingly chose the adult class.

The teacher was in her seventies and was using the prescribed Sunday School curriculum. The other adults had their books as well. I now understand that the only thing setting this teacher apart from her students was the TEACHER marking on the cover of her book. There is really no way she studied the content. She would read her teacher portion and then give her personal, mostly uneducated, and often unscriptural commentary.

The lesson was on heaven. The cherry on the top of this teaching fiasco came when one of the students asked how to earn a crown in Heaven. The teacher's response is forever imprinted on my mind. She said, "I wouldn't worry too much about earning a crown for

Heaven. All you are gonna do with it is throw it at Jesus' feet. He doesn't need it." She did not stop there! "I just focus on getting there, even if I barely skate in by the skin of my teeth." Close scene....

I think much more damage was done that morning through teaching than if we would have all climbed on the roof and thrown firecrackers at the late arrivals who had enough sense to bypass this particular Sunday School.

Middle ear hearing is necessary to be an effective teacher. If you don't spend time listening to God's voice while studying the scriptures, you will end up, much like the teacher in East Texas, inserting your own opinions into your lessons and calling it truth. Jesus was the master teacher. He taught his disciples the importance of listening to the voice of God: "But when he, the Spirit of truth, comes, he will guide you into all the truth. He will not speak on his own; he will speak only what he hears, and he will tell you what is yet to come," John 16:13 (NIV).

In Acts 18, we are introduced to Apollos. We learn that he boldly spoke the truth and was highly intelligent when it came to expounding upon the scriptures. But when he came across Priscilla and Aquila, they realized that his spiritual ears needed to be attuned: "Meanwhile a Jew named Apollos, a native of Alexandria, came to Ephesus. He was a learned man, with a thorough knowledge of the Scriptures. He had been instructed in the way of the Lord, and he spoke with great fervor and taught about Jesus accurately, though he knew only the baptism of John. He began to speak boldly in the synagogue. When Priscilla and Aquila heard him, they invited him to their home and explained to him the way of God more adequately." Acts 18:24-26 (NIV).

Most likely, the "way of God" explained was the baptism of the Holy Spirit. That fact is eluded to when it mentions that "he knew only the baptism of John." Upon finishing the lesson of this powerful teaching duo, Apollos joined the other disciples in Achaia. He was a great asset in winning public debates with the Jewish leaders concerning the true identity of Jesus. Remember, Paul tells us that for the Jews, Jesus was a stumbling block, and they needed to see the power of God. If Apollos had great success in winning over the Jews, he must have been displaying this empowerment through the Holy Spirit. God used Priscilla and Aquila to bring spiritual gain to his intellectual knowledge.

EXHORTATIONS WITH LOVE AND KINDNESS

Being a preacher's kid makes you privy to a lot of the inner workings of the church. I was raised in a Spirit-filled church where my father did a great job of facilitating the move of the Spirit while still maintaining balance and order.

A new couple in their late fifties began to attend the church. They were a sharply dressed and polite couple. He had a background of ministry, and they seemed like a nice fit. The church my dad was pastoring had just recently consolidated with another church and was rapidly growing.

About their third time to visit, the man, obviously sensing a personal move of the Spirit yelled out in a fantastically loud voice, "Shondi" (Shawn-die). That was it. No follow up, no interpretation, no anything.

Well, that was a surprise to everyone. I remember my parents discussing it on the way home that Sunday night. Then it happened again the next Sunday night and the talk on the way home was, "Let's have them over for dinner, and we can talk about it then."

Friday night came, and the couple arrived for dinner. I was twelve years old and relishing the conversation I knew would ensue. After dinner, I pretended to be doing something else other than listening in on the talk, but I assure you, I was all ears. My father kindly explained the workings of the Spirit and the gift of tongues and interpretation of tongues in a corporate setting. The man received the words his new pastor gave him and assured him he would discontinue the one-word hijacking of the service. There was a sense of relief in the house.

As our family escorted them to the door to say good night, my father was in a jovial mood after the apparent success of "the talk." He told one of his famous jokes on the porch, and the man did not laugh. He let out a booming "Shondi" on our porch.

The mood was at best awkward as they walked to their car. Well, that did not work....

It happened a couple more times in church, and this did not merit an invitation for dinner at the pastor's house but earned an invitation to Pastor's Office. I was not present at this meeting, but I do know it was much clearer and forthright with a couple of leaders from the church involved. The couple attended a few more weeks but left as quietly as they came. I call this season the "Shondi Showdown."

Healthy exhortation should involve encouragement. But encouragement may not involve exhortation. Exhortation carries with it a spurring on to greater works. When you spur a horse, you gouge its sides so that it runs at a swifter pace. That can be rather painful, but it also may be necessary if you are trying to outrun danger. Those with middle ear hearing can spur others on to greater works using just the right pressure so as not to bring injury.

Although he is gracious with his words, there is an urgent command in Paul's exhortation to the church in Thessalonica: "Now we ask you, brothers and sisters, to acknowledge those who work hard among you, who care for you in the Lord and who admonish you. Hold them in the highest regard in love because of their work. Live in peace with each other. And we urge you, brothers and sisters, warn those who are idle and disruptive, encourage the disheartened, help the weak, be patient with everyone. Make sure that nobody pays back wrong for wrong, but always strive to do what is good for each other and for everyone else." 1 Thessalonians 5:12-15 (NIV).

The Thessalonian church was newly established. However, they were in the midst of a major trade city that was also the seat of a military base. Paul had been run out of town, and he knew that the young church would also face persecution. Therefore, they needed the strength of loyalty to leadership, believers growing into maturity, and unified community. He needed to spur them on, so they moved from their reliance upon him into being a mature body of believers.

Learning to exhort in love and kindness takes time. If you feel as though you may never reach this level of maturity, know this: every believer has a maturing process designed to bring them to the Lord's desired end. Some early Pentecostal denominations gave out exhortation papers to new church leaders instead of licensing. They wanted to affirm the maturity of that leader before they set them in place as a licensed minister. There are some still today holding to that practice. This is not to hold people back, but rather to give them time to learn and grow. New preachers can be filled with passion yet lack the compassion that comes with walking through trials. Those with middle ear hearing not only know that God is holy, they hear his compassionate heartbeat for people in pain. Paul didn't hold back on the warnings, but he also said, "encourage the disheartened, help the weak, be patient with everyone."

INTERPRETING DREAMS AND VISIONS

The interpretation of dreams in ancient civilizations was considered an honored scientific profession. It was widely believed that certain intelligent men who were studied in the philosophies of the day could understand the symbolism in dreams and bring forth their meaning. Dreams were seen as communication from divine deities. The interpretation of these dreams often guided kings and governing officials in making important decisions that charted the course of history.[5]

Old Testament Dreamers

Although there were others, Daniel and Joseph are the supreme dream interpreters in the Old Testament. It would have been a normal occurrence for rulers in both Babylon and Egypt to seek out dream interpreters. What was not normal is the way in which these two men could answer their dignitaries: "The astrologers answered the king, "There is no one on earth who can do what the king asks! No king, however great and mighty, has ever asked such a thing of

---

[5] Hughes, J. Donald. (2000). Dream Interpretation in Ancient Civilizations. Dreaming. 10. 7-18. 10.1023/A:1009447606158.

any magician or enchanter or astrologer." Daniel 2:10 (NIV). In Daniel's case, Nebuchadnezzar didn't just want an interpreter, he wanted someone to tell him what he had dreamed, and then tell him the interpretation. If no one was found, all those that called themselves wise would be executed.

Although Pharaoh had shared his dream with his wise men, he was unsuccessful at finding one that could accurately interpret his dreams. As we discussed earlier, Joseph's ministry to Pharaoh's servant while in prison, had set the stage for Joseph to be brought to Pharaoh. By answering the questions no other wise man could answer, Joseph was promoted from the prison to Egypt's second commanding officer. (Genesis 40-41).

In both instances, these men relied upon God for the interpretations. It wasn't logical assumption or learned wisdom through philosophical books allowing these two dream interpreters to find favor with their perspective rulers. It was the way they relied on God and heard his voice that set the stage for two pagan rulers to encounter the Almighty.

New Testament Dreamers

There are many dreams recorded in the New Testament. During the trying of Jesus, Pilate's wife sent to him, saying, "Have nothing to do with this man, for I have suffered many things this day in a dream because of him," Matthew 27:19(NIV). Because Pilate feared man more than God, who was speaking to his wife, he did not follow this directive. History tells us he was demoted from his position and ended his career in disgrace.

Other dreamers in the New Testament were Jesus' earthly father, Joseph, the wise men, and the Apostle Paul. In all of the dreams these people had, there was no need for interpretation. They were direct and forthright lacking abstract symbolism.

I would caution against using dream interpretation books, manuals, and websites. Allow Holy Spirit to speak to you to help interpret dreams and visions which contain symbolism. The use of manufactured helps can cut God's Spirit out of the equation and put confidence in the product of a person.

Another word on dreams and visions: they come through personal time spent with the Lord. You must have an understanding of the Word. You also must understand what God's voice is like. They are addendum to our prayer life and Bible study. At best, they are guides and promptings to what we are already sensing in our spirits. I treat dreams and visions as confirmations.

We see this truth in Acts 10 as Peter experiences a vision that changes his perspective: "About noon the following day as they were on their journey and approaching the city, Peter went up on the roof to pray. He became hungry and wanted something to eat, and while the meal was being prepared, he fell into a trance. He saw heaven opened and something like a large sheet being let down to earth by its four corners. It contained all kinds of four-footed animals, as well as reptiles and birds. Then a voice told him, 'Get up, Peter. Kill and eat.'

'Surely not, Lord!' Peter replied. 'I have never eaten anything impure or unclean.' The voice spoke to him a second time, 'Do not call anything impure that God has made clean.' This happened three times, and immediately the sheet was taken back to heaven."Acts 10: 9-16 (NIV).

Peter knew Jesus. He had walked with him, talked with him, and learned from him. In his passionate nature, Peter had been willing to die for him. In his weakness, through denying who Jesus was, he had been humbled. But he had also been called to be foundational in establishing the Lord's Church.

Peter had already seen Gentiles come to a saving knowledge of Jesus when he preached on the Day of Pentecost. We do well to remember that the disciples were all devout Jewish men before Jesus arrived on the scene. In Peter's devotion, he was still adhering to the dietary restrictions given in the law. You see a glimpse into his intimate nature with Jesus in his reply to hearing the Lord's voice – he argued with him. I find that funny. But Jesus knew Peter. He knew how he processed, so he spoke to him again.

Peter needed confirmation in order to truly understand the wide reach of the Kingdom message.

The vision given to him was revolutionary to his belief system. The law of God that had always governed Jewish devotion was now obsolete in making one right before the Father. He had seen it before as he preached and now was being sent to the Gentiles with the good news. He experienced spiritual gain in his understanding of God's heart towards all people.

WORDS OF KNOWLEDGE AND WISDOM

My first pastorate is where I began to operate in words of knowledge and wisdom. I read books by Kenneth Hagin, Kenneth Copeland, and Marilyn Hickey as I began to hunger for the workings of spiritual gifts in my life.

A young family began attending infrequently. After a few weeks, they came to a healing service we conducted. They always sat in the back and never participated in praise and worship. During this particular service, the father brought their young son to the front to be prayed over. He had a club foot, and God did a miraculous work. The boy's foot immediately straightened when we prayed. The father was overcome with joy but could not coax his wife to the front to see what was happening with their son.

They had never attended a Wednesday evening service. The Wednesday following the miracle, the mother showed up by herself and moved forward a few rows. At the end of the Bible study, I invited people to come forward to kneel and pray at the altars. The young mother remained glued to her seat. Very clearly, the Lord impressed upon me she had been sexually abused by relatives as a child and had impactful trust issues which were controlling her life. This was a word of knowledge. I silently prayed and then followed the Spirit's prompting.

A few weeks earlier, one of the ladies in the church shared her story of childhood sexual abuse at the hands of male uncles and cousins. She was extremely honest about her life and the fallout it had caused her. She was in attendance this Wednesday night. I went to her quietly and asked if she would share her personal story with this young lady. She did so, and I saw the lady respond with many tears. As they talked and prayed, God gave the storyteller a word of wisdom for the young mother regarding her future if she would but trust God. The lady immediately gave her heart to Jesus, and the family began to regularly attend and participate in the ministries of the church.

Words of knowledge reveal information from a person's past up until the present. Words of wisdom have to do with the future. Fortune tellers, charlatans, and psychics traffic in words of knowledge because a person's past is known in the spirit world. The same group of people cannot operate in words of wisdom. They will usually veer to necromancy, or talking to the dead, in order to bring information of a departed loved one. By doing so, they play on the emotional vulnerability of their victim. This is demonic and a complete counterfeit of the gifts of the word of knowledge and wisdom.

A word of knowledge should not serve as a stand-alone gift. This can easily turn into a form of entertainment. For the one receiving the word, it becomes flesh-building. For the one giving the word, it can become a source of pride. Jesus showed us the proper way to minister in words of knowledge and wisdom when he addressed the Samaritan woman at the well.

Jesus was alone as he sat down by Jacob's well. It was custom that the women would come at specific times of day to gather water and fellowship with one another. However, this woman that showed up at noon seemed to want to avoid the crowd. When he asked her for water, it must have been a shock to her senses:"The Samaritan woman said to him, "You are a Jew and I am a Samaritan woman. How can you ask me for a drink?" (For Jews do not associate with Samaritans.)" John 4:9 (NIV).

Jesus begins his dialogue with a veiled discussion on his true identity. He gently exposes her true need as he speaks of his ability to give her living water. Her response reveals the shame in her heart, "The woman said to him, "Sir, give me this water so that I won't get thirsty and have to keep coming here to draw water." John 4:15 (NIV). In other words, if she had such a thing as living water, she could avoid the crowd that gathered at the well. He prompted her to go get her husband, but she tells him that she is not married. It is here that Jesus uses a word of knowledge to open her heart to what he had to say. Jesus said to her, "You are right when you say you have no husband. The fact is, you have had five husbands, and the man you now have is not your husband. What you have just said is quite true." John 4:17-18 (NIV).

The woman is still grappling with her shame as she acknowledges Jesus as a prophet. Why would she see him as such? Because a word of knowledge had revealed the truth of her circumstances. He probably told her even more about herself that wasn't recorded. But she reminded him that the Jewish tradition would not recognize her sacrifices as true worship because of her heritage as a Samaritan and her inability to worship in Jerusalem.

The compassion of Jesus would not leave her in this exposed condition. He continued to lead her into truth with a word of wisdom: 'Woman,' Jesus replied, 'believe me, a time is coming when you will worship the Father neither on this mountain nor in Jerusalem. You Samaritans worship what you do not know; we worship what we do know, for salvation is from the Jews. Yet a time is coming and has now come when the true worshipers will worship the Father in the Spirit and in truth, for they are the kind of worshipers the Father seeks. God is spirit, and his worshipers must worship in the Spirit and in truth.'" John 4:21-24 (NIV).

From here, Jesus no longer veils his identity. He tells her plainly that he is the Messiah. Her sense of shame must have been broken because she rushed into the crowd that just minutes before, she had avoided. She became a great evangelist that day as the crowd followed her to meet their Savior. The story ends with many coming to a saving knowledge of the truth.

We can see that a word of knowledge is used to get the attention of the person needing a word of wisdom. This is where the clairvoyant ensnares unwitting people. They share something from their past which is privy to the spirit world. The person is amazed and listens to anything they say at this point as truth. From there, the psychic leads the participant into deception. A mature Christian, operating in words of knowledge and wisdom, will lead the participant into redemptive truth.

MIDDLE EAR AILMENTS

Vertigo can be experienced from both inner and middle ear issues. Cholesteatoma[6] is one condition that causes vertigo. Irregular skin growth in the middle ear, behind the eardrum, begins to form. This is rather common in people who experience repeated, chronic ear infections.

Spiritual disorientation (vertigo) in middle ear hearing comes from a constant bombardment of worldliness. We allow our minds to become engrossed by what fuels the lust of the eyes, the lust of the flesh, and the pride of life (chronic infection). In exchange, we live somewhat mixed in our motives which creates confusion and a loss of clarity in our hearing. When this occurs, we are unable to maintain proper balance, and our perception of what is real and solid (the truth of God's word) is disrupted. We have to stop and assess

---

[6] Heathline Editorial Team, *Cholesteatoma: Causes, Symptoms, and Diseases,* Healthline Media: (2019)
https://www.healthline.com/health/cholesteatoma#causes (accessed November 21, 2018).

what is causing the confusion and examine it against what the Scripture says, asking the Holy Spirit to reveal all false beliefs and idols we may have set up for ourselves.

If this spiritual condition is not remedied, we will not be effective in how we minister to people. The spiritual gain that we received in order to grow into someone with middle ear hearing will begin to diminish. We must learn to obey God's will even when our flesh or our soul desires otherwise. The beloved apostle John tells us:"Do not love the world or anything in the world. If anyone loves the world, love for the Father is not in them. For everything in the world—the lust of the flesh, the lust of the eyes, and the pride of life—comes not from the Father but from the world. The world and its desires pass away, but whoever does the will of God lives forever." 1 John 2:15-17 (NIV).

OBEDIENCE FACTOR

Remember outer-ear hearing does not require a great amount of obedience. But, in order to maintain its gain, middle ear hearing requires immediate obedience to God's voice at the level of one's understanding. A common issue that must be overcome is having a sense of halting obedience due to the fear of man. Paul knew this to be true as he wrote, "Am I now trying to win the approval of human beings, or of God? Or am I trying to please people? If I were still trying to please people, I would not be a servant of Christ." Galatians 1:10 (NIV).

At this level of hearing, a marriage of being attuned to God's voice and a knowledge of the Scriptures has taken place. We have learned how he speaks to us and how he directs us. If we succumb to being afraid of total obedience due to what others may think or say, we begin to replace Father's voice with the limited opinion of others. This may provide us a sense of safety, but it will not take us to the place of maturity that God wants for each of his children.

Be encouraged! You don't have to know all of this at once. If you truly desire to mature and you spend time in prayer and Bible study listening for the Lord's voice, you are on the right path. He knows just the right pressure to spur you on into maturity.

INNER EAR HEARING

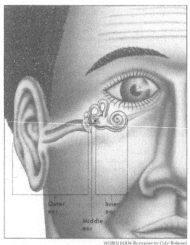

WORLD BOOK illustration by Colin Bidgood
The human ear extends deep into the skull. Its main parts are (1) the outer ear, (2) the middle ear, and (3) the inner ear.

Figure 3 [7]

Did you know the inner ear stretches deep into the structure of the face, sitting directly under your eye? Your cheekbone actually protects the inner components of your hearing. There are two main parts of the inner ear: the cochlea, which enhances hearing, and the vestibular system, which strengthens balance. The cochlea is divided into two chambers and is filled with thick fluid and small

---

[7] World Book illustration by Colin Bidgood, "The human ear." *The World Book Encyclopedia* © 2019. By permission of the publisher. www.worldbook.com All rights reserved. This illustration may not be reproduced in whole or in part in any form without prior written permission from World Book, Inc.

hair-like cells attached to the outer membrane. These hair-like cells push the sound through the fluid. This changes the sound waves into an electrical current.

The second function of your inner ear involves the labyrinthine or semi-circle canals. This determines the position of the head which aids in balancing the entire body. Both processes are sent through the auditory nerve to the brain so that the information can be interpreted. It is in the brain where sound is processed and understanding occurs.

The auditory nerve is actually a bundle of nerve fibers. This nerve is joined with the vestibular nerve, becoming what is known as the 8th cranial nerve. Running alongside this is the facial nerve, which allows for facial expression and sensory processing. All of these nerves work together to communicate to the brain. But what is most interesting is that the brain communicates back to the inner ear through these nerve fibers as well. As many as two-thirds of the nerve fibers actually carry sound back to the cochlea.[8] The cochlea

---

[8] Alberti, P. W. (2001). The anatomy and physiology of the ear and hearing. *Occupational exposure to noise: Evaluation, prevention, and control*, 53-62.

takes the processed information and uses it to suppress the sounds that you are not needing in that particular moment. This is why you can zone in on one conversation while tuning out what you don't want to hear. Not only is this an important function of physical inner ear hearing, it defines what it means to have inner ear hearing on a spiritual level.

Literary works often portray owls as the epitome of wisdom. But when one studies the natural abilities of owls, a picture is painted of tremendous tenacity and an uncompromising focus. These intense predatory birds lock onto the sound frequency of their prey through their amazingly heightened hearing abilities. The shape of their heads actually acts like a satellite dish that collects sound. Like the inner ear of a person that suppresses sound not needed, owls can tune out the noise of wind or other elements and listen for small animals scurrying about. Once it hears an animal moving under a pile of leaves, fallen branches, or snow, it uses its sensitive hearing to hunt it down and snatch it from its hiding place.

Again, like our inner ear components, an owl's ears are located by its eyes. Once the sound frequency of a scurrying animal catches the owl's attention, both the head and the eyes are essentially locked onto its prey. The thrust of an owl's wings is soundless so that nothing interferes with its listening. Its eyes and head remain focused on the exact spot that the frequency is picked up, even if it has to fly through trees or other barriers. Once the owl reaches the exact location of the noisy animal, its hiding place is no match for the predatory bird. Its deadly talons are pointed in the exact spot of the sound, and more often than not, the owl comes away with its dinner. If it has to circle around and come back, it is still locked onto the sound frequency.[9] This is why farmers love to have owls take up residence in their fields. They keep the rodent population to a minimum.

I have my own experience in witnessing the tenacity of owls. A few years ago, I was having our home built in a rural, heavily wooded area with a creek running behind it. Since moving in, our family has seen deer, bobcats, skunks, opossums, armadillos, rabbits, squirrels and a menagerie of birds.

I would go by and check on the progress of the house at least once a day. After the house was nearing completion, with windows inserted and electricity turned on, I would sometimes go at night. One

---

[9] Joy Lanzendorfer, *"15 Mysterious Facts About Owls,"* Mental Floss (2015), http://mentalfloss.com/article/68473/15-mysterious-facts-about-owls (Accessed November 3, 2018).

particular autumn evening, I went into the house and heard a banging in the master bedroom. There were no cars or trucks remaining at the house, so I was unsure of the source of the noise. I turned the light on in the bedroom in time to see a small owl crash into the bay window facing the woods. By the looks of things, this looked like an ongoing saga. (I thought it was a juvenile owl. With the convenience of a google search, I later found out this was an adult eastern screech owl. In my search, I also found out, due to their ferocity, they are often called "feathered wildcats."

The owl was totally exhausted from repeated attempts of escaping into the woods. (Knowing what I know now about their forceful tenacity, I realize we have extremely durable windows.) Since I assumed this was a young owl, I assumed I could talk it down. My wife has often laughed at me and called me an "animal whisperer." My efforts were not in vain on this particular night. The feathered wildcat finally stopped bashing into the window as I continued to gently talk to it. I assured the owl I would gently give it freedom if it would allow me to help it. I did have moments of apprehension as I keyed in on its talons and beak.

After about five minutes, the owl resigned, and I gently picked it up and slowly walked it through the house and out the back door, all the while softly talking to it. As soon as we hit the cool evening air, the owl lifted from my hands and both silently and swiftly disappeared into the large trees.

Tenacity, singularly-focused, and the ability to completely surrender to the Holy Spirit are defining characteristics of one with inner ear hearing on a spiritual level. A person hearing at this degree has hyper-sensitive processing when it comes to listening to God's voice. Just like the owl calmed down when he heard my voice, a person with inner ear hearing has learned to surrender to God's. There is a single-minded approach of locking onto the frequency of heaven that drowns out all other noise. These people have been schooled in the ways of the Spirit and can bring forth God's directives with clarity and precision.

Inner ear hearing, in essence, is tuning out all demonic or earthly distraction in order to understand and bring forth the deep revelation of the Spirit. This revelation brings heavenly strategy to either rout demonic forces or decree the will of God.

When the kingdom that had been ruled by Saul was ready to be handed over to David, God brought armed men from every tribe to surround him. We don't think much about it as we read these stories in the Bible, but the spiritual warfare surrounding David was probably severe. Yes, God had decreed that David would be king, but certainly that had to raise the ire of spiritual opposition. In 1 Chronicles 12, we see a list of those men who swore their allegiance to their newly crowned king. Of all the tribes that were mentioned, God says this about the sons of Issachar, "... men who understood the times and knew what Israel should do." 1 Chronicles 12:32 (NIV).

Out of twelve tribes, the sons of Issachar were the only ones spoken of this way. From this, we can likely determine that there are less than 10% of believers who ascribe to inner hear hearing today – even in a church setting of strong prophetic people. They are not more special than others. They simply have been spiritually trained in unusual ways, often through continual warfare or dire circumstances. Like the owl, their senses are locked onto the sounds coming from the throne and they do not easily veer in any other direction.

DEEPER REVELATIONS OF THE SPIRIT FOR THE CHURCH

Those with inner ear hearing often hear what the Spirit is saying to the corporate Church today. This goes beyond what God is saying to me personally and is broader than a word given in a Sunday morning setting. This message carries with it the weight of God's decreed will for his people.

We see this with the Apostle John as he wrote the book of Revelation. It was common for the Roman Empire to imprison those they deemed as political prisoners. The Roman Emperor Domitian would command heads of household to acknowledge him as deity. Those who refused were often banished to remote islands and sentenced to forced labor. Most likely, this was the reason John was sent to the island of Patmos where he had his apocalyptic vision.

John was given revelation for seven different churches in Asia. "On the Lord's Day I was in the Spirit, and I heard behind me a loud voice like a trumpet, which said: 'Write on a scroll what you see and send it to the seven churches: to Ephesus, Smyrna, Pergamum, Thyatira, Sardis, Philadelphia and Laodicea.'" Revelation 1:10-11 (NIV). While in the Spirit, John turned to see who was speaking to him and encountered Jesus in his glory and splendor. The disciple, who was known as the beloved, fell on his face in reverence. Jesus gave him clear instruction to write down the revelation that he received so that each church could hear their assigned directives.

We also see this kind of activity throughout history as God enlightened men and women to bring revelation to His Church where darkened mindsets attempted to prevail. Many gave their very lives to live out the truth of what had been entrusted to them from God's throne. Romans 1:18 speaks of truth being suppressed. Dark spiritual forces, along with man's finite understanding, will continually try to dilute the truth that sets men free, but God has his remnant who hear nothing but the frequency of heaven. These people will boldly obey the voice of God so that others may know of God's love and redemption no matter the cost to themselves.

The history of Europe is filled with stories of people who radically obeyed God in the midst of religious persecution. Many times, I have traveled to the Czech Republic. Every time I leave the beautiful city of Prague, I think of the next time I can return. There is something special about that city which intrigues me. There is an over-abundance of castles, whimsical cathedral spires and intricate towers looming over the red tiled roofs that always causes me to ponder life in centuries past. I have many times become lost meandering through the narrow cobblestone streets of the Mala Strana. I have spent hours wandering through the castle gardens and parks of the Hradcany District and solemnly walked the streets of the Josefov, the former Jewish ghetto. All these places have intimate coffee shops, bakeries and hearty Bohemian kitchens to get lost in as well.

The highlight of each visit is the archaic beauty of Old Town Square. I always book a room in a hotel which was formerly a Franciscan monastery built in the fourteenth century with a view of the expansive square. In the middle of the view, and in front of the Tyn Cathedral, stands a memorial monument to John Huss (Jan Hus), considered the first church reformer.

John was born into a humble Bohemian family in 1374. To escape poverty, he trained for the priesthood and was ordained in 1401 after completing his schooling at Charles University in Prague. He would continue to serve in the same city as the lead preacher at Bethlehem Chapel, which would pack in three thousand people to hear his sermons.[10]

---

[10] James E. Kiefer, "John Huss, Priest and Martyr, 6 July 1415," Biographical Sketches of Memorable Christians of the Past, (1999) http://justus.anglican.org/resources/bio/7.html

John studied the works of John Wycliffe and fell in love with the Bible. He railed against the selling of indulgences instituted by numerous popes and eventually riled the emotions of the king who received a portion of the indulgences. Huss was banished from his church and eventually prosecuted and indicted by the Church as a heretic.

After he was sentenced to death, he was stripped of his priestly rights and robes and was turned over to the secular authorities. Further humiliation followed with a tall paper hat placed on his head with the inscription, "Haeresiarcha" (i.e., the leader of a heretical movement). Next, strongmen led him to a stake where the executioner undressed him, tied his hands behind his back with a rope, and chained his neck to the stake, which was surrounded by straw and wood up to his neck.

At the last moment, he was asked to recant and thus save his life. He declined and said:

(accessed December 6, 2018).

"God is my witness that the things charged against me I never preached. In the same truth of the Gospel which I have written, taught, and preached, drawing upon the sayings and teachings of the holy doctors, I am ready to die today."

According to some accounts, when his life was coming to a close, he cried out, "Christ, son of the Living God, have mercy on us!" His ashes were thrown into the Rhine River to prevent the veneration of his remains.

His memory lived on, and in 1621, twenty-seven Protestant leaders were executed for their role in the failed Bohemian Rebellion against the ruling pro-Catholic Habsburg Monarchy. In front of Prague's Old Town Hall are 27 white crosses, worked into the gray cobblestones of the Old Town Square, commemorating their martyrdom.

PROPHESYING TO MOVEMENTS AND NATIONS WITH AUTHORITY

Our own Pentecostal history can be defined as a renewal of the endowment of power given through the Holy Spirit. Because the Church had become politicized and institutionalized, the Baptism of the Holy Spirit had been suppressed throughout the church age. What had begun in an upper room in Jerusalem had become nominalized as Christianity became a pawn for nationalism instead of the good news for all nations.

Charles Fox Parham is known as "the Father of the Pentecostal Movement." His deep desire to recover this experience of Pentecost caused him not only to receive the Baptism of the Holy Spirit in the same manner as in Acts, but to prophesy it into existence for others.

Charles was born in Muscatine, Iowa on June 4, 1873. From the time of infancy, Charles dealt with varying debilitating diseases, as well as continual struggles. His mother died when he was only seven years old. He felt the call of God on his life as a young boy but did not come to a saving knowledge of Christ until he was thirteen. He struggled with the thought of living a life of poverty as a minister, which caused him to consider a different vocation. But upon what physicians called his death bed due to rheumatic fever, he called out to Jesus for deliverance. He received his healing as he surrendered to preach the Gospel.

He continued to receive healing in dramatic ways which solidified his message that healing was inherent to the Gospel. The intensity of his experiences with God's healing power only served to create a deep hunger for more of the Spirit. He would often stand and declare that entire communities would be taken for God's glory.

It seemed that Charles Parham would be an easy choice for a pastorate in the local denominational church, but his spiritual appetite often put him in conflict with what was the religious norm. The religious leaders that surrounded him maligned his name and as he is said to have announced, "I left denominationalism forever, though suffering bitter persecution at the hands of the church who seemed determined if possible, my soul should never find rest in the world or in the world to come. Oh, the narrowness of many who call themselves the Lord's own."[11]

His insatiable hunger for the recovery of what was then known as Apostolic Faith is what led him to become the pioneering father of Pentecostalism in the first decade of the 1900s. Reports of receiving the Baptism of the Holy Spirit were growing. There were even rumors of individuals receiving the gift of tongues on occasion. All of this helped him determine that God desired the Holy Spirit to be

---

[11] Goff, James R, *Charles F. Parham*, The New International Dictionary of Pentecostal and Charismatic Movements, 2002; James R. Goff, *Fields White unto Harvest: Charles F. Parham and the Missionary Origins of Pentecostalism* 1988.

poured out upon his Church much like Peter proclaimed in Acts. He desired a recovery of suppressed spiritual gifts and felt as though there was a great end-time harvest of souls that would take place if regained.

He also knew that missionaries needed to know the language of the people they encountered. He believed that the spiritual gift of tongues would allow them to speak whatever language was needed in the country they felt called to reach. This caused him to form a team of forty students that diligently studied the Bible to determine what the evidence was for receiving the Baptism of the Holy Spirit. The unanimous decision the students formed was that although there was not a formula in obtaining the blessing, the evidence was that each recipient spoke in other tongues.

As a student at Parham's Bethel Bible College in Topeka, Kansas, on January 1, 1901, Agnes Ozman was the first person recognized as receiving "the baptism of the Holy Spirit with the evidence of speaking in tongues." From here, groups of ministers began receiving the same through the "laying on of hands." With great elation, Parham is reported to have asked for the blessing himself. "Then he asked God for the same blessing, and when he did, Parham distinctly heard God's calling to declare 'this mighty truth to the world. And if I was willing to stand for it, with all the persecutions, hardships, trials, slander, scandal that it would entail, He would give me the blessing.' It was then that Charles Parham himself was filled with the Holy Spirit and spoke in other tongues."[12]

Prophesying to churches, movements, and nations with authority requires that you are locked onto the frequency of heaven no matter the cost. Inner ear hearing allows one to be so enamored with the things of God that nothing else satisfies. This ability is often honed through great trial and affliction, but the training to hear God's voice in such a way is vital if that one is going to be used to make public proclamations on this level. Decreeing God's will often involves recovering truth that has been suppressed. To be trusted in the Christian community, you have to have a proven track record for people to listen to you more than once.

Modern prophets often take much flak from the church at large because of the subjective nature of prophetic ministry. However, the litmus test that can be given is to have this proven track record. Dr. Marilyn Hickey can certainly be called an evangelist. But she is also adept at prophesying to nations.

---

[12] Ibid

EXPERIENCING OPEN VISIONS

Because of this ability to hear God's voice with clarity, those with inner ear hearing do not always need others to interpret their heavenly encounters. What they hear and what they see are synced together. Their senses are heightened to God's voice and they know his ways. The sixth chapter of Isaiah is a defining moment in the life of the prophet. Many a song has been written about Isaiah's open vision. However, the imagery wasn't only about God inhabiting the temple and the prophet knew it. "In the year that King Uzziah died, I saw the Lord, high and exalted, seated on a throne; and the train of his robe filled the temple. Above him were seraphim, each with six wings: With two wings they covered their faces, with two they covered their feet, and with two they were flying. And they were calling to one another: 'Holy, holy, holy is the Lord Almighty; the whole earth is full of his glory.' At the sound of their voices the doorposts and thresholds shook, and the temple was filled with smoke." Isaiah 6:1-4 (NIV). Words are not used arbitrarily in the scriptures. The key phrase in this passage of scripture is, "In the year that King Uzziah died, I saw the Lord..."

In the book of Second Chronicles, we learn that King Uzziah began to reign in Jerusalem when he was sixteen. (2 Chronicles 26:3-5). He reigned two years and as long as he sought the Lord, God blessed him with prosperity. Not only does the Bible tell us of Uzziah's accomplishments, but archeological digs reveal that what Uzziah built is most likely more extensive than what is credited to Hezekiah.[13] But Uzziah's heart became full of his accomplishments, and we learn, "But after Uzziah became powerful, his pride led to his downfall. He was unfaithful to the Lord his God and entered the temple of the Lord to burn incense on the altar." Only the priests were to burn incense on the altar. It is in this moment that King Uzziah is struck with leprosy and an earthquake hits Jerusalem believed to have split the Mount of Olives. The historian Josephus records damage to the temple that allowed a ray of light to shine upon the king's face revealing his leprous condition.[14] In light of these events, Isaiah receives his call. The role of prophet in ancient Israel was often linked directly to the ruling king. Yet, there are

---

[13] Steven M. Ortiz, (2009), "Urban city planning in the eighth century: a case study of recent excavations at Tel Gezer (reading between the lines: Uzziah's expansion and Tel Gezer)," *Review & Expositor* 106, no. 3: 361-381., *ATLA Religion Database with ATLASerials*, EBSCO*host* (accessed December 15, 2018).

[14] Julian Morgenstern, (1937), "Amos studies II the sin of Uzziah, the festival of Jeroboam and the date of Amos." *Hebrew Union College Annual* 12-13, 1-53, *ATLA Religion Database with ATLASerials*, EBSCO*host* (accessed December 15, 2018).

only two kings whose annuls are said to be written by prophets.[15] One is Abijah who was memorialized by Iddo. The other is Uzziah. It is the prophet Isaiah that chronicles Uzziah's history.

What King Uzziah had done in the temple demanded a response from the Lord, so that the people would honor God over their beloved king. Isaiah saw the Lord's glory and heard the worshipping angels proclaiming holy, holy, holy. This was a profound moment that Isaiah carried with him the rest of his days. As he wrote of the king's accomplishments to be passed down throughout history, he was careful to record the low points as well. Not to bring dishonor to Uzziah, but to give full glory to the one "high and exalted, seated on the heavenly throne." He lived within the context of receiving his open vision and knew what God was communicating.

INTERPRETING YOUR OWN DREAMS

In the previous chapter, we saw that Peter needed the interpretation of his dream to be made clear. But when we first meet Joseph in

---

[15] Eliezer Livneh, (1960) "Prophecy and monarchy: religion and state in the biblical era," *Tradition* 2, no. 2: 262-272, *ATLA Religion Database with ATLASerials*, EBSCO*host* (accessed December 15, 2018).

Genesis 37, we are led to believe that the boy was an avid dreamer and understood for himself what his heavenly experiences meant from childhood. "One day, Joseph told his brothers what he had dreamed, and they hated him even more. Joseph said, "Let me tell you about my dream. We were out in the field, tying up bundles of wheat. Suddenly my bundle stood up, and your bundles gathered around and bowed down to it." Genesis 37:5-7 (NIV).

Although his immaturity was on display, so was his ability to lock onto the frequency of heaven. He may not have understood the context of his dream, but he knew that one day his brothers would indeed bow down to him. Joseph's ability to interpret dreams is unmatched except by Daniel. As we have already seen, God used Joseph throughout his adulthood to interpret the dreams of others so that God might be made known to the ruling powers of the day.

However, I can't help but think that it was his boyhood dream that he clung to as he endured great turmoil because of his spiritual tenacity. Restitution for the jealous behavior that he aroused might have been his initial motive for wanting to see the actualization of his dream. But, by the time the fulfillment came, his immaturity had given way to deep compassion. His brothers truly did bow down to him, but Joseph didn't use the opportunity to gloat – he wept tears instead. God had placed him in a position to save his family from certain death. The process had been full of pain and rejection, but he had learned to forgive and simply serve however the Lord needed.

AUTHORITY OVER REGIONAL AND NATIONAL STRONGHOLDS

"No weapon forged against you will prevail, and you will refute every tongue that accuses you. This is the heritage of the servants of the Lord, and this is their vindication from me," declares the Lord." Isaiah 54:17 (NIV).

The Bible is full of warfare language. Most of these battle verses come with promises of victory and equip us for the ensuing fight that every believer will face to some degree. Sometimes, however, we see that God's people allowed an enemy to take ground that was not theirs to take, such as the case in Lamentations: "The kings of the earth did not believe, nor did any of the peoples of the world, that enemies and foes could enter the gates of Jerusalem" Lamentations 4:12 (NIV).

God had brought his people out of bondage in dramatic fashion. He had taken them through the wilderness to train them on how to trust him and completely obey. He had established them in the land

and promised that if they adhered to his ways, nothing could uproot them from their inheritance. And yet, we read in Lamentations that the whole world watched as their enemies came through the gates and took Jerusalem.

Spiritually speaking, a personal stronghold is a mindset that has been set-up by the devil to bring deception, and ultimately, captivity. When speaking of regional or national strongholds, this entails an entrenched lie within a people group that strengthens the devil's agenda to rob, kill, and destroy. We can see a myriad of strongholds within our own nation. Most notably, the fact that abortion is not only legal throughout all nine months of pregnancy, but highly celebrated.

Inner ear hearing allows a person, or group of people, to successfully battle the spiritual forces in operation that keep people in captivity. The person trained in this kind of warfare has typically had their own share of battles that required radical obedience to overcome. They have learned not to lean on their own understanding and that their physical strength is no match for the cosmic battle that rages. Instead, they lock all their senses upon heaven, knowing that it is God's divine strategy that is needed in order to break the prevailing mindsets so that others may find freedom.

As a prophetic church, we have fought many a battle with demonic forces. One in particular comes to mind as it pertains to authority over regional or national strongholds. Our church offices are located in a shopping center. When we first moved our sanctuary into this location, the offices next to us where rented out by Planned Parenthood – the largest providers of abortion in the world. We knew that we couldn't share space with a place that deceives and brings harm to people. We would repeatedly go after business hours to lay hands on the doors and pray for their removal. God heard our prayers. Now our pastoral offices are in the same space that Planned Parenthood vacated. My personal office is the very room where the abortions took place. When the landlord remodeled, I asked that the sink would remain as a testimony to the Spirit's ability to break strongholds and rout the enemy out.

Understanding the authority, the Lord has given us is vital for one with inner ear hearing. Paul teaches us, in the book of Ephesians, the wisdom needed to successfully win spiritual skirmishes: "For our struggle is not against flesh and blood, but against the rulers, against the authorities, against the powers of this dark world and against the spiritual forces of evil in the heavenly realms." Ephesians 6:12 (NIV). Jesus didn't defeat Satan through earthly wisdom. He won the war as he willingly laid down his life. Because of Jesus' sacrifice, our enemy is a defeated foe and knows his time is short. But while he still roams the earth, Satan attempts to deceive as many as he can. As Christians, we use the authority given us by Jesus when we walk in confident assurance that we can successfully wage war against demonic forces in any place Satan rears his ugly head. Because of Jesus' victory – all of heaven backs us up!

SPIRITUAL AILMENTS

In my early twenties, I had a case of Labrynthitis. This is a viral infection of the inner ear which causes vertigo. Vertigo is a sense of feeling off balance. It manifests in one of two ways. The first way vertigo can affect you is to make you feel as though you are spinning. Vertigo can also make you feel like the world around you is spinning. Because the inner ear regulates not only the ability to hear sound, but the ability to balance, I was in bad shape!

I had experienced mild bouts of dizziness for a couple of days; nothing nauseating, simply bothersome. I was at church on a Sunday night and opened one of the swinging doors into the auditorium. At that moment, a wave of vertigo overtook me. I could not stand up straight but instead, fell back into the wall, catching the door. Not only was I completely disoriented, the crash of the door was loud! It took several minutes for my head to clear.

If we do not understand the authority Christ has given, we can have a similar sense of spiritual imbalance. We can feel as though we are reeling from spiritual attacks that bring disorientation and confusion. There is a continual sense that we are falling backward instead of hearing God's strategy to take new ground for the kingdom. The devil's goal is to make us feel like we are going around and around in a revolving door of the same struggles, instead of experiencing the abundance of life that Father has for his children that is truly just on the other side of the door.

Inner ear hearing ailments also include complete hearing loss. This happens when the hair-like cells found in the cochlea are damaged because of excessive noise. Remember, the hair-like cells actually serve to push sound waves through the fluid within the inner ear. We can liken this process to a strong current pushing against seaweed in the ocean. Just as seaweed can be broken off by constant pressure, these cells can be damaged in the same way.

Sometimes, the hair-like cells simply stop moving and can be repaired by prolonged rest from the offending level of sound.

However, once these cells are broken off, they will not grow back. This causes permanent hearing loss that can only be treated through a cochlear implant.[16]

Carrying offense in your heart is the spiritual equivalent to extreme noise that seeks to take away your inner ear hearing. The frustration and pain that have built up act like a throbbing pain that hinders your ability to focus on anything but your offense; in this way, the noise of your hurt threatens to impede your ability to hear the things of God. It becomes not just a distraction, but all-consuming.

Through this constant warfare, the believer is made more aware of their inner turmoil than the throne room of heaven. Once lies are lodged into one's thinking, that person is in a state of constant emotional charge. Inner ear hearing is then lost because the perception of reality is skewed. Negative circumstances begin to define truth instead of what God has decreed from His throne.

---

[16] Mandy Mroz, AuD, *"Types of Hearing Loss,"* Your Hearing Network, (2019) https://www.healthyhearing.com/help/hearing-loss/types (Accessed May 10, 2019).

If we find ourselves in this kind of heightened internal pain, we must seek God's healing through absolute surrender. This means that we forsake holding onto any offense whether it seems justified or not. He can restore any and all permanent damage and heal us completely. He also knows how to silence the noise of our pain and retune our ears to his voice.

Most scholars attribute the writing of Psalm 91 to Moses. He certainly had his share of extreme offense. He had obeyed God in radical fashion only to find himself at odds not only with Pharaoh, but with the very people he had been called to lead out of bondage. Like Jesus, he was acquainted with sorrow, but he also knew where to run for much needed shelter. "Whoever dwells in the shelter of the Most High will rest in the shadow of the Almighty. I will say of the Lord, "He is my refuge and my fortress, my God, in whom I trust." Surely, he will save you from the fowler's snare and from the deadly pestilence. He will cover you with his feathers, and under his wings you will find refuge; his faithfulness will be your shield and rampart." Psalm 91:1-4 (NIV).

CONCLUSION

"Silence is golden. It can also drive you crazy."
Michael Hedrick, Ph.D.; Professor at California State University

If you are like me, then there are days you want to get away from it all. In the 1980's and 1990's there was a bubble bath product, named Calgon, that advertised heavily on television. The commercials were all the same theme; highlighting the difficulties of domestic life. In the advertisement, the frazzled housewife would be shown juggling an escalating list of problems until she would exasperatingly utter, "Calgon, take me away!" The next scene would show her in a quiet room luxuriating in a bath full of bubbles in blissful abandon.

I may not understand the complexities of a 1980's era housewife in need of a relaxing bath escape, but I do know when I need quiet. Sensory overload happens when one or more of the body's senses is overwhelmed by the environment. In today's world, there are innumberable things competing for the control of our senses; especially sight and sound.

Some people need noise to concentrate. I am the opposite, I need quiet; but not for too long. Too much quiet can also prove stressful. The *Daily Mail* published an article on the quietest place on Earth: The Anechoic Chamber at Orfield Laboratories in Minneapolis, USA. This special room blocks 99% of all external sounds using 3.3 feet of fiberglass, acoustic wedges, double walls of insulated steel and a foot of concrete.

One would think this is a great place of retreat. Surprisingly, no one has succeeded in staying in the room for more than forty-five minutes due to hallucinations from the quiet. Steven Orfield, the company's founder, told the *Daily Mail*: "When it's quiet, ears will adapt. The quieter the room, the more things you hear. You'll hear your heart beating, sometimes you can hear your lungs, hear your stomach gurgling loudly. In the anechoic chamber, you become the sound."[17] It sounds like a freaky episode of Rod Sterling's *Twilight Zone*. No thank you...I will pass!

In the Apostle Paul's Second letter to the Corinthian believers he wrote of awaiting the new body. In 2 Corinthians 5:6-7 the author writes, "Therefore we are always confident and know that as long as we are at home in the body we are away from the Lord. For we live by faith, not by sight." Be careful not to become too "at home" in your body. That is when we tend to trust what we naturally see more than what we spiritually hear.

The three fallacies of sight: *Seeing is Believing, I Can See in the Dark* and *My Eyes Never Play Tricks on Me* are all tied to the natural ways of handling life. This is what Paul was warning the Corinthian saints about. Our natural eyesight is tied to our natural (carnal) mind.

---

[17] Michael Hedrick, *Silence is golden. It can also drive you crazy,* The Week (2013) https://www.theweek.com/articles/460780/silence-golden-also-drive-crazy (Accessed July 8, 2019).

Spiritual hearing is imperative to an overcoming spiritual life. For a believer, not hearing from God can become a deafening silence much akin to Minnesota's Anechoic Chamber. The silence can become deafening. We hear sounds of our own doubt and fear which can easily lead to depression and anxiety.

Dare to hear the voice of your Heavenly Father. There is a wonderful promise in Jeremiah 33:3, "Call to me and I will answer you and tell you great and unsearchable things you do not know." I believe this is a blessing extended to every believer. We must simply access this promise. Ask Father to speak to you. Start where you are at. There is nothing wrong with Outer Ear Hearing. Start there and press in to hear more.

Promotion into Middle Ear Hearing is a wonderful transition. It happens through desire to hear God's voice more clearly in a personal and tangible way. Prayer at this stage becomes more about listening. This is the stage of God answering us when we call him, as laid out in Jeremiah 33:3.

Moving from Middle Ear Hearing into Inner Ear Hearing is where Almighty God tells us "great and unsearchable things we do not know." This is the place of great revelation. This is where your life is truly transformed from "self" to "serve."

For too long the Church has reserved Inner Ear Hearing for the spiritually elite. It does not take great spiritual strength nor the "right" religious pedigree. Hearing from God does not depend on who you know or how well connected you are to those of importance in the Church world. It is about HIM!

John recorded his vision in the Book of Revelation. In Chapter 3, verses 7-8 he records, "To the angel of the church in Philadelphia write: These are the words of him who is holy and true, who holds the key of David. What he opens no one can shut, and what he shuts no one can open. I know your deeds. See, I have placed before you an open door that no one can shut. I know you have little strength, yet you have kept my word and have not denied my name."

It does not take a lot of strength to hear, just be quiet before the Lord. The Door of Inner Hearing has been opened for you. Enter in....

ABOUT THE AUTHOR

John Bates has served in full-time ministry for more than thirty years. He is the senior leader of Freedom Fellowship International in Waxahachie, Texas; part of the South Dallas Corridor. This is a body known for a strong prayer emphasis. The church oversees multiple campuses in Egypt and Honduras as well. The people of Freedom facilitate over fifteen international ministry trips per year. The church specializes in conducting Freedom Quests for the Nations, equipping church leaders to break generational strongholds and walk in true freedom.

John is the president of John Bates Ministries, a global presence conducting signs and wonders services, leading prayer festivals along with planting churches while equipping and ministering to church and world leaders. He operates predominantly in the gifts of faith, words of knowledge/wisdom and the working of miracles. Marilyn Hickey Ministries is a Global Miracle Ministry and she has personally given him the moniker, "Profitable Prophet."

For many years he has served on the board of Global Initiative: Reaching Muslim Peoples and on the President's Council of the

Assemblies of God Theological Seminary. John enjoys partnering with other ministries and is known as a bridge builder. He also serves as consultant to several ministries and businesses.

John and Shelli Bates have been married for over twenty-five years and are the parents of two young adults: Nehemiah and Eden. The Bates live in the Dallas area.

www.JohnBatesMinistries.com

ACKNOWLEDGMENTS

I would like to thank:

Brad and Julie Duncan for your kind and generous support and sweet friendship.

Kristene O'Dell for helping me get thoughts out of my head and onto paper.

Amy George for your extraordinary editing skills.

Ken and Ellie Gates for believing in me and continually letting me know it.

Phil and Deniese Geery for your timely prayers.

Dawana Quintana for pushing me further with your questions.

Cory Lucas, Michael Holmes and Jason Morgan for listening ears.

Nehemiah Bates for the on-point cover design.

Valerie Wilson and Anika Janelle Pettiford for pulling it all together.

Pastor Scott Wilson for fleshing out the ideas of this book with me and allowing me to share them with The Oaks Fellowship.

The people of Freedom Fellowship International for living the book with me and for allowing me to be me!

Other books by John Bates

Spread the Fire: Making Room for God

Can your church be both seeker-friendly and Spirit-filled? In Clear the Stage, John Bates and Scott Wilson share how God gave them a vision to marry these two divergent streams of church practice. You don't have to choose between the old revivalist mentality and the more recent seeker-sensitive plan. Instead, the authors present a whole new way of doing church that clears the stage so the Spirit of God can do what only He can.

Spread the Fire: Spirit Baptism in Today's Culture

Today's church is hungry for supernatural moves of God. In Spread the Fire, John Bates and Scott Wilson invite you, the pastor, or church leader to a new level of training, teaching and modeling Spirit-filled living. It's likely you already address vital topics like forgiveness, integrity and reaching the lost, but teaching about the fullness of the Holy Spirit must also be woven into daily church life. Through Spread the Fire, you will ignite the flame by sharing testimonies of supernatural tongues, signs and wonders, prophecy and other divine moves of God. With Spread the Fire, you will become equipped to lead a Spirit-empowered church!

JOHN BATES

Thanks for reading! Please add a short review on Amazon and let me know what you thought!

Made in USA - Kendallville, IN
64295_9780578517223
01.19.2022 1611